off the shelf

about the author

Donna Hay is an Australian-based food stylist, author and freelance food writer. Her work appears in newspapers and magazines, and she is well known for the four cookbooks she produced for *marie claire* – *marie claire cooking*, *marie claire dining*, *marie claire food fast* and *marie claire flavours* (published internationally as *The New Cook*, *New Entertaining*, *New Food Fast* and *Flavours*, respectively) – which have brought her global success.   Awards and nominations to date: for *flavours*, The Guild of Food Writers Awards 2000 (UK) – Cookery Book of the Year; Glenfiddich Award (UK) – Best Cook Book 2001; James Beard Foundation/Kitchen Aid Book Awards (USA) – nominee for Best Food Photography 2001. For *dining*, Jacob's Creek World Food Media Awards (Aust) – Gold Award – Best Soft Cover Recipe Book 1999; Australian Food Writers' Award 1999 (Aust) for Best Soft Cover Recipe Book. For *cooking*, International Association of Culinary Professionals Cookbook Awards (USA) (formerly the Julia Child Cookbook Awards) – The Design Award 1998.

thank you

As far as art directors go, I know I have the best: Vanessa Holden – never predictable, always challenging and inspiring; I am so lucky to have you as my best friend, too. Con Poulos, thank you for being so easy to work with and for making this book so beautiful; your love of food and homemade wine has added a unique twist. Ben Masters and Briget Palmer, the most dedicated chefs I could ask for – you make it all so much easier; thank you for your enthusiasm and your damn hard work. Didee Bull and Paula Berge, thank you for keeping the business running and the props rolling; you both keep me sane. Foong Ling Kong – such a swift, capable and efficient editor – perfect! Lucy Tumanow-West – a great editor and an even better storyteller. At HarperCollins, publisher Shona Martyn, Helen Littleton, Russell Jeffery, Judi Rowe, Jill Donald and Christine Farmer – thank you for your energy and enthusiasm.   Thanks to Billy the Butcher, my much-loved partner, who came close to strangling me while I was doing this book but managed to hang in there. And my family, who always get the raw deal – thank you for still loving and supporting me. Ellie, Sibella, Heidi, Chris and Brad, who have contributed to the book in one way or another. And also my friends, big and small, for the love and light relief: Elisha, Gabby, Simon, Yasmin and Jody, and Toby for his coffee.   Shelly at Mud Australia – just when I think I've seen the most beautiful ceramics in the world, you come up with more. For all the wonderful props from Le Creuset, Pillivuyt @ Hale Imports, Boda Nova, Royal Doulton, Wheel & Barrow, Dinosaur Designs, Jarass, and Wabi Gallery. Tony Lee and Smeg appliances, Profiline cookware, KitchenAid, Sunbeam and Braun for my kitchen equipment. Thank you to my suppliers for the best produce and their good advice and good humour: Anticos Fruitworld, Demcos Seafoods and Paddington Fresh Foods.

First published in Australia in 2001
by HarperCollins*Publishers* Pty Limited
First published in Great Britain in 2001
by Fourth Estate
A Division of HarperCollins*Publishers*
77–85 Fulham Palace Road
London W6 8JB
www.4thestate.co.uk

3 5 7 9 10 8 6 4 2

A catalogue record for this book is available from the British Library.

ISBN 1 84115 770 8

Cover photograph: Summer pasta. For recipe, see page 30
Film by Colorwize Studio, Adelaide, South Australia
Produced by Phoenix Offset on 157gsm Chinese Matt
Printed in China

off the shelf

donna hay

photography by con poulos

contents

introduction

Your pantry shouldn't just be where half-used ingredients go to dry out. Nor should it be the final resting place of sad old jars of mustard ('Well, I think it's mustard…'), those packets of spices you've only ever used a teaspoon of, and the various tubes of exotic pastes that have only been squeezed once (and there's no way you'll ever remember the recipe you bought them for).

With *off the shelf*, I'm giving you the tools to reinvent your pantry and your approach to cooking. I want you to think about what's in your cupboards as the bones of your cooking, the stuff you really need. Each chapter explores and explains the truly essential ingredients you will actually use, such as pasta, rice and canned tomatoes, and the basics that will get you by on those days you wake with the desire to bake. With this information in mind, you can tailor your own pantry to suit, and only stock the ingredients you'll need to make the food you enjoy cooking and eating. More information about ingredients and basic recipes marked with an asterisk* can be found in the glossary.

The secret to getting the most out of your pantry basics is to use well-chosen fresh ingredients. Think of your cupboard as your basic cooking wardrobe, with the fresh ingredients providing the dynamic accessories that highlight the season, provide colour and texture, and really give you the opportunity to make a dish your own.

I use the ideas in *off the shelf* to make sense of my own frantic kitchen. Hope you can too. Enjoy!

olive
English mustard
2x cans white beans
        ↳ cannellini

can chick peas

                    capers
lemon   pepper
2 x limes

baby spinach
asparagus

Recipes 2000

- lamb cutlets
- 8 slices pancetta
- 4x eye fillet

Shopping list

These items are optional extras. Depending on what you like to cook and eat, you may want to complete your pantry with some of them. When stocking up, think of your refrigerator and freezer as companions to your pantry – together, their contents are your cooking essentials.

herbs
thyme
rosemary
oregano

Dried herbs are generally no substitute for fresh ones, although they are better than nothing. Don't keep dried herbs for any longer than 6 months, as they lose their flavour, and choose dried leaves rather than ground herbs. Only use dried herbs in cooked dishes, never in raw foods such as dressings or salads. When cooking, use a quarter of the amount of dried herbs as you would fresh herbs.

spices
ground cumin
ground coriander
star anise
cinnamon
nutmeg
vanilla beans
black peppercorns
sea salt

Spices are essential for flavouring foods, and the following should make up your basics. For Asian cooking, you'll need cinnamon and star anise. Cumin and coriander provide a complex, earthy spice flavour. Nutmeg is also a handy ingredient; buy it whole and grate it as you need it rather than buying it pre-ground. Always keep some vanilla beans on hand. Split the beans, scrape out the seeds, and add both to your cooking for vanilla flavour that is superior to vanilla extract. Stock some cinnamon sticks, which can be used whole or ground for their pungent flavour. Choose dark black peppercorns for their aromatic qualities, and good-quality sea salt for its flavour and purity.

freezer
peas
broad (fava) beans
frozen berries

Even though I am a strong advocate of fresh rather than frozen food, there are a few freezer essentials. Basic vegetables such as peas and beans can be added to soups, risotto and pasta dishes. And for easy baking in any season, keep frozen raspberries, blueberries and blackberries, which can be baked unthawed.

ice-cream

Quality vanilla bean ice-cream is perfect alone and with most desserts.

ready-prepared puff + shortcrust pastry

Keep sheets or slabs of pastry ready to be thawed and used. Top puff pastry with sliced fruit and bake for a simple dessert galette. Line a tart tin with shortcrust and add a sweet or savoury filling for an easy weekend meal.

stock

An absolute essential, either in TetraPak form or frozen in tubs. Great as a base for soups and stews, and to boost the flavour of sauces and meat dishes. Use chicken, beef and maybe vegetable stock as the foundation for quick meals. To make a warming and filling soup, simmer sliced chicken, chopped vegetables and small pasta in some chicken stock, and season.

refrigerator
cheddar
parmesan
+ one you love
ricotta

Cheeses are great to have on standby for a simple cheese sandwich, or over pasta or in a risotto. Keep cheddar, parmesan and perhaps one of your favourites, such as a blue or soft cheese on hand. If you love the creaminess of ricotta, either to toss through hot pasta with some rocket (arugula) or to bake in a cake, keep some in the refrigerator but remember it has a short shelf-life.

milk
cream
thick cream
butter
yoghurt

Milk is a must – whether to make a quick custard or simply to enjoy in a strong morning coffee. Keep cream to enrich a sauce or to pour over a dessert. If you don't have the time to whip it yourself, buy some thick cream to spoon over desserts. Butter is a must, not only to spread on hot toast, but also for those times when the baking urge takes hold. Yoghurt is *the* breakfast solution and can also be made into a quick minted dipping sauce. Or simply sprinkle some brown sugar over thick plain yoghurt to accompany fruit or just about anything.

and the rest
coffee
tea
jam

Coffee's not only for drinking – this wonderful dark liquid can also be poured over ice-cream to make 'affogato' or sweetened to a syrup for pouring over hot cake. Nothing is better than a cup of tea with a simple afternoon snack; keep a range of herbal teas to complement different foods. Raspberry, apricot or whatever – with jam in the cupboard a piece of bread can be transformed into a sweet treat. Or spread between layers of cake and serve with warm custard.

fettuccine
pappardelle
ziti

pasta

spaghetti
linguine
angel hair
maccheroni
orecchiette
penne
rigatoni

basics

wide
fettuccine, pappardelle, ziti

A simple rule – big pasta needs a big sauce! These thick, flat shapes are best with robust, well-flavoured sauces that are in balance with the pasta. Serve with cream-based, browned butter, meaty or rich tomato sauces.

thin
spaghetti, linguine, angel hair

Great for thin or oil-based sauces which will coat each strand of pasta. These types of pasta work well with most sauces but are particularly suited to seafood such as clams or simple flavours like herbs, chilli, garlic and lemon.

short
maccheroni, orecchiette

Because short pasta is smaller and somehow more dense, it is ideal for chunky vegetable sauces such as broccoli and asparagus. Cut the vegetables just a little bigger than the pasta. Short pasta is great for soups and broths.

round
penne, rigatoni

These wide shapes, with or without ridges, are easily coated and are good for holding meaty, tomato or cheese-based sauces. They make a great base for baked pasta dishes topped with meat and tomato or spinach and ricotta sauce.

tricks + tips

perfect pasta

For perfect results cook pasta in plenty of rapidly boiling water. It's important to keep the water boiling, so after adding the pasta, give it a quick stir and then return the lid to the saucepan for 3 minutes or until the water returns to the boil. Remove the lid and stir the pasta again. Cook the pasta until it is al dente – just cooked through but still with some bite.

oil free

There is no need to add oil to the cooking water when preparing pasta. It doesn't really prevent the pasta from sticking together, as it just floats on the surface of the water. To stop pasta from sticking, it must be added to rapidly boiling water and then stirred to separate the strands. Be sure the water continues to boil throughout the whole cooking process.

the drain

When draining pasta, use a large colander and shake well to remove all the excess water. If the pasta is waterlogged it will dilute the sauce. When draining tube-like pasta such as rigatoni or ziti you may need to stir it in the colander to remove all the cooking water. If using the pasta cold, rinse it under cold water to remove excess surface starch so that it doesn't stick together.

staying warm

When combining cooked pasta with a sauce, it is best to keep them both as hot as possible before serving. A simple way to do this is to return the drained pasta to the pot it was cooked in and then toss through the hot sauce. This keeps the pasta hotter than if it was combined with the sauce in a separate serving bowl.

pasta with pumpkin and sage brown butter

pasta with pancetta and peas

spaghetti with garlic clams

pasta with pumpkin and sage brown butter

1 kg (2 lb) pumpkin, peeled and diced
olive oil
400g (14 oz) pappardelle or fettuccine
75g (2¹/₂ oz) butter
3 tablespoons whole sage leaves
1 cup finely grated parmesan cheese
cracked black pepper and sea salt

Preheat the oven to 190°C (375°F). Place the pumpkin in a baking dish and sprinkle with a little olive oil. Bake for 30 minutes or until golden and soft.
Just before the pumpkin is ready, cook the pasta in a large saucepan of lightly salted boiling water until al dente. Drain. While the pasta is cooking, place the butter and sage in a saucepan over low to medium heat and allow the butter to simmer until a golden brown colour.
To serve, place the pasta in serving plates and top with the pumpkin and parmesan. Spoon over the brown butter and sage leaves and season with pepper and salt. Serves 4.

pasta with pancetta and peas

400g (14 oz) pasta such as penne
1 kg (2 lb) peas in the pod, or 300g (10 oz) shelled peas
1 tablespoon butter
1 tablespoon oil
12 slices pancetta*, sliced
¹/₂ cup shredded mint leaves
¹/₄ cup chopped flat-leaf parsley
¹/₂ cup grated parmesan cheese
cracked black pepper

Place the pasta in a large saucepan of lightly salted boiling water and cook for 10–12 minutes or until al dente. Drain. While the pasta is cooking, place the peas in boiling water and blanch for 2 minutes, then drain.
Heat a frying pan over medium to high heat. Add the butter, oil, peas and pancetta and cook for 4 minutes or until the pancetta is crisp. In a large serving bowl, toss the pea mixture with the pasta, mint, parsley, parmesan and pepper. Serve immediately. Serves 4.

spaghetti with garlic clams

1 tablespoon olive oil
8 sprigs thyme, halved
4 cloves garlic, sliced
1 tablespoon grated lemon zest
1 kg (2 lb) clams (vongole), scrubbed and rinsed
¹/₂ cup (4 fl oz) white wine
400g (14 oz) spaghetti
1 tablespoon butter
1 tablespoon chopped flat-leaf parsley
cracked black pepper and sea salt
lemon wedges to serve

Heat a deep frying pan over medium heat. Add the oil, thyme, garlic and lemon zest and cook for 2 minutes or until fragrant. Add the clams and wine, cover and cook for 3 minutes or until the clam shells have opened.
Cook the spaghetti in a large saucepan of lightly salted boiling water until al dente. Drain and place in a serving bowl. Toss the spaghetti with the butter, parsley, pepper and salt. Pour the clams over the spaghetti and serve with lemon wedges. Serves 4.

pasta with tomato, basil and olives

400g (14 oz) fettuccine or ziti
1 tablespoon olive oil
1 onion, chopped
2 cloves garlic, crushed
2 x 400g (14 oz) cans peeled tomatoes
¹/₃ cup roughly chopped basil
¹/₄ cup sliced black olives
cracked black pepper and sea salt
pinch sugar
parmesan or goat's cheese to serve

Cook the pasta in a large saucepan of lightly salted boiling water until al dente. Drain.
While the pasta is cooking, heat a large frying pan over medium heat. Add the oil, onion and garlic and cook for 4 minutes or until lightly golden. Add the tomatoes, crush them lightly with a fork and simmer for 4 minutes. Stir through the basil, olives, pepper, salt and sugar. Toss the sauce with the pasta and serve topped with parmesan or goat's cheese. Serves 4.

pasta with tomato, basil and olives

19

lemon chicken pasta

pasta with chilli, tomato and mozzarella

pasta with mushrooms

lemon chicken pasta

400g (14 oz) spaghetti or linguine
3 tablespoons olive oil
3 tablespoons salted capers*, rinsed
2 cloves garlic, sliced
2 small red chillies, seeded and chopped
3 cooked chicken breast fillets, shredded
1 tablespoon grated lemon zest
3 tablespoons lemon juice
1 cup chopped basil leaves
salt and pepper
1/2 cup grated parmesan cheese

Place the pasta in a large saucepan of lightly salted boiling water and cook until al dente. Drain.
While the pasta is cooking, heat a deep frying pan over high heat. Add the oil, capers, garlic and chillies and cook for 1 minute. Add the chicken and lemon zest and cook, stirring, for 4 minutes or until the chicken is heated through. Add the pasta to the pan with the lemon juice, basil, salt and pepper and toss to combine. Place in serving bowls and top with parmesan. Serves 4.

pasta with chilli, tomato and mozzarella

1 tablespoon olive oil
1 onion, chopped
2 cloves garlic, sliced
2 small red chillies, seeded and chopped
2 x 440g (141/2 oz) cans peeled tomatoes
400g (14 oz) rigatoni or penne
2 tablespoons chopped oregano
cracked black pepper and sea salt
200g (7 oz) fresh mozzarella or bocconcini, sliced

Heat a frying pan over medium heat. Add the oil, onion, garlic and chillies and cook for 3 minutes or until the onion is soft. Add the tomatoes and crush with a fork. Simmer for 3 minutes.
While the sauce is cooking, place the pasta in a large saucepan of lightly salted boiling water and cook until al dente. Drain.
Add the oregano, pepper and salt to the sauce. Toss the sauce through the pasta and place in serving bowls. Serve topped with mozzarella. Serves 4.

pasta with mushrooms

2 tablespoons butter
1 red chilli, seeded and chopped
400g (14 oz) sliced mushrooms, such as field, shiitake or button
3/4 cup (6 fl oz) vegetable stock
3/4 cup (6 fl oz) cream
2 tablespoons lemon juice
400g (14 oz) fettuccine or linguine
1/2 cup finely grated parmesan cheese
1/4 cup chopped basil
cracked black pepper and sea salt

Heat a frying pan over medium heat. Add the butter, chilli and mushrooms and cook for 4 minutes or until the mushrooms are brown. Add the stock, cream and lemon juice and simmer for 5 minutes.
While the sauce is simmering, place the pasta in a large saucepan of lightly salted boiling water and cook until al dente. Drain. Toss the pasta with the mushroom sauce, parmesan, basil, pepper and salt. Serves 4.

spinach and ricotta baked pasta

500g (1 lb) rigatoni
2 bunches (750g/11/2 lb) English spinach, stems removed ■
750g (11/2 lb) fresh ricotta
300 ml (10 fl oz) sour cream
4 eggs, lightly beaten
1 cup grated parmesan cheese
2 tablespoons chopped dill
cracked black pepper and sea salt

Preheat the oven to 180°C (350°F). Cook the pasta in a large saucepan of lightly salted boiling water until al dente. Drain. Place the pasta in a well-greased 4 litre (8 pint) capacity baking dish.
Blanch the spinach in a saucepan of boiling water, drain and squeeze to remove excess liquid. Roughly chop the spinach and place in a bowl. Add the ricotta, sour cream, eggs, parmesan, dill, pepper and salt and mix to combine. Spoon the mixture over the pasta. Bake for 25–30 minutes or until golden. Stand for 5 minutes before cutting into wedges. Serve with a simple tomato salad. Serves 6.
■ You can also use 375g (12 oz) frozen spinach, thawed and drained to remove excess water. You should have around 150g (5 oz) cooked spinach.

spinach and ricotta baked pasta

spaghetti with asparagus and lemon cream

1¹/₂ cups (12 fl oz) cream
1¹/₂ cups (12 fl oz) chicken stock
1 teaspoon grated lemon zest
¹/₄ cup (2 fl oz) lemon juice
³/₄ cup finely grated parmesan cheese
400g (14 oz) spaghetti
500g (1 lb) asparagus, trimmed
¹/₄ cup chopped flat-leaf parsley
cracked black pepper and sea salt

Place the cream, stock and lemon zest in a frying pan over medium heat and allow to simmer rapidly. Gradually whisk in the lemon juice, then stir in the parmesan and cook for a further 10 minutes or until the sauce has thickened. Place the spaghetti in a large saucepan of lightly salted boiling water and cook until al dente. Drain.
Cut the asparagus into thirds and steam over boiling water until tender.
To serve, toss the spaghetti with the asparagus, lemon cream, parsley, pepper and salt. Serves 4.

pasta with simmered veal shanks

6 thick slices veal shank
2 x 400g (14 oz) cans peeled tomatoes, crushed
4 cups (1³/₄ pints) beef stock
1 cup (8 fl oz) red wine
2 cloves garlic, sliced
2 tablespoons chopped thyme leaves
cracked black pepper and sea salt
400g (14 oz) rigatoni or penne
parmesan cheese to serve

Place the veal shanks, tomatoes, stock, wine, garlic, thyme, pepper and salt in a deep frying pan or large saucepan and bring to the boil. Cover and simmer over low to medium heat for 45 minutes or until the veal is tender.
Remove the veal from the pan. Simmer the sauce, uncovered, and reduce until it thickens. Remove the meat from the bones and chop.
Cook the pasta in a large saucepan of lightly salted boiling water until al dente. Drain. Mix the veal into the sauce and toss the pasta through. Place on serving plates and top with parmesan. Serves 4.

pasta and broad bean minestrone

4 ripe tomatoes, quartered
5 cups (2 pints) chicken or vegetable stock
1 tablespoon olive oil
2 onions, finely chopped
3 stalks celery, chopped
4 rashers bacon, chopped
2 cups or 300g (10 oz) shelled broad (fava) beans ▪
150g (5 oz) small soup pasta*
cracked black pepper and sea salt
¹/₃ cup shredded basil
8 slices crusty bread
olive oil, extra
¹/₃ cup finely grated parmesan cheese

Place the tomatoes and 2 cups (16 fl oz) of the stock in a blender and purée until smooth. Pour the mixture through a sieve and set aside.
Heat a large saucepan over medium to high heat. Add the oil, onions, celery and bacon and cook for 8 minutes or until the onions are soft. Add the tomato mixture, remaining stock and broad beans to the pan and simmer for 12 minutes. Add the pasta, pepper and salt and cook for a further 10 minutes or until the pasta is soft. Stir through the basil.
To serve, drizzle the bread with a little oil. Sprinkle lightly with parmesan and grill (broil) until golden. Ladle the soup into bowls and serve with the parmesan toasts. Serves 4.
▪ You can use frozen broad beans but you will need to peel them.

pasta with buttered broccoli

1 kg (2 lb) broccoli, cut into small florets
400g (14 oz) orecchiette or penne
1 tablespoon olive oil
2 tablespoons butter
2 cloves garlic, sliced
2 red chillies, seeded and chopped
1 tablespoon shredded lemon zest
cracked black pepper and sea salt
parmesan and lemon wedges to serve

Steam the broccoli over boiling water for 4 minutes or until tender. Set aside.
Cook the pasta in a large saucepan of lightly salted boiling water until al dente. Drain.
While the pasta is cooking, heat a frying pan over medium heat. Add the oil, butter, garlic, chillies and lemon zest and cook for 2 minutes. Add the broccoli, toss to combine and heat through. Toss the broccoli mixture with the pasta, pepper and salt. Place on serving plates and serve with parmesan and lemon wedges. Serves 4.

spaghetti with asparagus and lemon cream

pasta and broad bean minestrone

pasta with simmered veal shanks

pasta with buttered broccoli

spaghetti and lemon-marinated salmon

penne with wilted rocket and salami

spaghetti and lemon-marinated salmon

600g (20 oz) salmon fillet, skin removed
3 tablespoons lemon juice
1 tablespoon olive oil
400g (14 oz) spaghetti, linguine or fettuccine
1 tablespoon olive oil, extra
3 tablespoons salted capers*, rinsed
1 cup grated parmesan cheese
1/4 cup roughly chopped flat-leaf parsley
cracked black pepper

Cut the salmon into small dice and place in a bowl with
the lemon juice and olive oil. Refrigerate for 30 minutes,
stirring once.
Place the pasta in a large saucepan of lightly salted boiling
water and cook until al dente. Drain.
Heat a frying pan over medium heat. Add the extra oil
and capers and cook for 3 minutes or until crisp. Toss
the pasta with half of the parmesan and the capers and
place on serving plates. Toss the salmon with the
remaining parmesan, the parsley and pepper, spoon
over the pasta and serve. Serves 4.

penne with wilted rocket and salami

400g (14 oz) penne
300g (10 oz) spicy salami or chorizo sausage, sliced
2 tablespoons salted capers*, rinsed
2 cloves garlic, sliced
200g (7 oz) rocket (arugula), stems removed and leaves halved
200g (7 oz) goat's cheese, sliced
cracked black pepper

Cook the pasta in a large saucepan of lightly salted boiling
water until al dente. Drain.
While the pasta is cooking, heat a frying pan over
medium to high heat. Add the salami and cook, stirring,
for 4 minutes or until crisp. Add the capers and garlic and
cook for 1 minute. Add the rocket and toss until wilted,
then remove from the heat. Toss the salami and rocket
mixture through the pasta and place in serving bowls.
Top with goat's cheese and pepper. Serves 4.

short order

pine nut brown butter

cherry tomato

simple zucchini

short order

pine nut brown butter

Cook 400g (14 oz) pappardelle or fettuccine until al dente, then drain. Melt 85g (2¾ oz) butter in a frying pan then add ½ cup pine nuts to the pan and simmer until the pine nuts are golden. Add pepper and sea salt and toss through the hot pasta. Finish with grated parmesan and serve as a simple meal or side dish.

cherry tomato

Cook 400g (14 oz) rigatoni or penne until al dente, then drain. Melt 60g (2 oz) butter in a non-stick frying pan over medium heat. Add 2 cloves sliced garlic and 350g (11½ oz) cherry tomatoes and cook, stirring, for 8 minutes or until tomatoes are soft and golden. Add a handful of chopped basil and then toss through the hot pasta. Sprinkle with balsamic vinegar, cracked black pepper, sea salt and grated parmesan.

simple zucchini

Cook 400g (14 oz) spaghetti or linguine until al dente, then drain. Heat a frying pan over high heat. Add 2 tablespoons olive oil, 2 seeded and chopped red chillies and 2 cloves crushed garlic and cook for 2 minutes. Add 3 grated zucchini (courgette) to the pan and cook for 2 minutes. Toss through the hot pasta and serve sprinkled with cracked black pepper, sea salt and shaved parmesan. Serve with lemon wedges.

zesty

Cook 400g (14 oz) orecchiette or penne until al dente, then drain. Over medium heat fry 2 tablespoons shredded lemon zest, 2 tablespoons rinsed salted capers, ½ cup flat-leaf parsley leaves and 2 chopped red chillies in ¼ cup (2 fl oz) olive oil until the parsley is crisp. Toss through the hot pasta and serve as a side dish or with added parmesan and shredded rocket (arugula) for a simple meal.

toasted crumb

Cook 400g (14 oz) spaghetti until al dente, then drain. Heat a frying pan over medium heat. Add 3 tablespoons olive oil, 2 cloves crushed garlic and 8 anchovy fillets and cook for 1 minute. Add 1½ cups fresh breadcrumbs and cook, stirring, for 5–7 minutes or until golden. Toss through the hot pasta with chopped parsley.

baked carbonara

Cook 400g (14 oz) ziti or fettuccine until al dente, then drain. Cook 4 chopped rashers bacon until crisp. Whisk together 4 eggs, 2 cups (16 fl oz) cream, 1½ cups (12 fl oz) milk and ½ cup grated parmesan cheese. Place pasta in an 8 cup (4 pint) capacity ovenproof dish and top with the bacon and the egg mixture. Bake in a preheated 180°C (350°F) oven for 30 minutes or until set.

summer pasta

For a taste of summer, roast halved cherry tomatoes until soft. Toss with cooked spaghetti and some chopped chilli fried in olive oil, baby rocket (arugula) leaves, and crisp grilled prosciutto if you like. Season with cracked black pepper and sea salt and serve.

tuna and lemon

Cook 400g (14 oz) pasta until al dente, then drain. Toss with 400g (14 oz) drained canned tuna, 3 tablespoons lemon juice, 2 tablespoons olive oil, ¼ cup chopped flat-leaf parsley and 1 finely sliced red onion. Sprinkle with cracked black pepper and sea salt and serve.

rocket and ricotta

Cook 400g (14 oz) fettuccine until al dente, then drain. Toss ricotta, baby rocket (arugula) leaves, pepper and sea salt through the warm pasta. Serve with a squeeze of lemon juice and grated parmesan if you wish.

zesty

toasted crumb

baked carbonara

summer pasta

tuna and lemon

rocket and ricotta

31

arborio
carnaroli
rice
jasmine
basmati
short grain.

basics

basmati

One of the family of long-grain fragrant rices. This rice has a slightly nutty flavour and a low starch content, so even when cooked by the absorption method the grains stay separate, making it perfect for pilafs and other dishes where the rice needs to be fluffy. The fragrance of this rice is particularly suited to Indian foods or foods with a similar spice base.

arborio or carnaroli

A medium-grain plump-looking rice grain that contains surface starch. When this rice is cooked until al dente the surface starch creates a cream from the stock it is cooked in, making a true risotto. Rice for risotto varies in quality, which greatly affects the finished dish. I prefer carnaroli rice for its superior creaminess when cooked.

short grain

This is a great standard rice for a multitude of dishes from baked rice puddings to sushi rice. Short-grain rices have enough starch for the grains to just cling together when cooked by the absorption method. Unlike the long-grain rices, short-grain rice has no distinct fragrance, making it very versatile.

jasmine

A fragrant and slightly perfumed long-grain rice used mainly in or to accompany Chinese, Thai and Vietnamese-style dishes. Jasmine rice contains enough starch for the grains to stick together when cooked by the absorption method. This quality makes the rice easy to eat with chopsticks. Do not add salt, as it destroys the delicate perfume.

tricks + tips

perfect cooking

I find the absorption method of cooking rice the easiest and most successful. The rice is cooked in a volume of water that will be completely absorbed during cooking; it will not need draining. Place the rice and water in a saucepan with a well-fitting lid and cook over medium to high heat for 8–10 minutes. A simple guide is 1 cup short-grain rice to 1 1/2 cups (12 fl oz) water and then 1 cup (8 fl oz) water for each additional cup of rice. For long-grain rice use 2 1/4 cups (18 fl oz) water for the first cup of rice and 1 1/2 cups (12 fl oz) water for every additional cup of rice.

stick or separate

When short-grain, long grain and jasmine rice are cooked by the absorption method, the grains stick together, which makes them easier to eat with chopsticks. These rices are perfect to serve with Asian foods and Thai curries. Basmati rice, the exception, has a low amount of starch, so even when it is cooked by the absorption method the grains remain separate.

wash or not

If you want rice grains to remain separate after cooking, you may want to wash the rice before cooking. This is essential for a fluffy, well-flavoured pilaf.

freeze leftovers

Cooked rice only lasts for three days in the refrigerator, so you may want to freeze leftover rice in sealed plastic containers or plastic bags with excess air removed. See Short Order on page 48 for quick recipes using leftover cooked rice.

rice cooker

If you serve a lot of foods with rice or use lots of rice in cooking, you may want to think about investing in a rice cooker. They vary in size and price, and produce perfect rice every time. Some rice cookers have a 'keep warm' setting that will ensure the rice stays warm after the cooking time is finished.

the risotto debate – bake or stir

There have been many debates over whether a risotto is a risotto if it hasn't been cooked on the stovetop and stirred throughout the cooking time to develop the creamy starch that risotto-type rices possess. For the time-poor, baking risotto is a good technique and the results are surprising. Baked risotto works better if good-quality carnaroli rice is used. At the end of cooking time the risotto will still be quite liquid. To develop the creamy starch in the risotto, you will need to stir for 3–4 minutes to get a thick consistency.

sweet pork fried rice   baked pumpkin and pancetta risotto

Thai lemongrass rice salad

sweet pork fried rice

1/2 cup (4 fl oz) hoisin sauce
1/3 cup (2 1/2 fl oz) Chinese cooking wine or sherry
1 tablespoon shredded ginger
500g (1 lb) pork fillet or tenderloin, trimmed and sliced
soy sauce to serve
rice
2 tablespoons peanut oil
4 spring onions (scallions), sliced
1 red chilli, seeded and chopped
6 cups cooked rice
8 leaves bok choy, halved lengthwise ■

Place the hoisin sauce, cooking wine and ginger in a frying pan over medium to high heat. Allow to boil for 2 minutes or until the mixture thickens slightly. Add the pork to the pan and cook, stirring, for 5 minutes or until cooked through and coated with the sauce. Set aside.
To make the rice, heat a deep frying pan or wok over high heat. Add the oil, spring onions and chilli and cook for 1 minute. Add the rice and cook, stirring, for 5 minutes. Add the bok choy and cook for 3 minutes.
To serve, place the rice in serving bowls and spoon over the pork mixture. Serve with soy sauce on the side. Serves 4.
■ If you don't have any bok choy, use green beans or asparagus.

baked pumpkin and pancetta risotto

2 cups arborio or carnaroli rice
5 cups (2 pints) chicken or vegetable stock
60g (2 oz) butter
500g (1 lb) jap or butternut pumpkin, peeled and finely diced
12 slices pancetta
3/4 cup finely grated parmesan cheese
cracked black pepper and sea salt
1 tablespoon chopped flat-leaf parsley

Preheat the oven to 200°C (400°F). Place the rice, stock, butter and pumpkin in an ovenproof dish and cover tightly with a lid or aluminium foil. Bake for 30 minutes or until the rice is soft – the risotto will be quite liquid.
While the risotto is cooking, place the pancetta under a hot grill (broiler) and cook for 2 minutes on each side or until crisp. Set aside.
Add the parmesan, pepper, salt and parsley to the risotto and stir for 2 minutes to thicken it. To serve, place in serving bowls and top with the pancetta. Serves 2.

Thai lemongrass rice salad

2 tablespoons peanut oil
2 stalks lemongrass, finely chopped
2 small red chillies, seeded and chopped
4 spring onions (scallions), sliced
4 cups cooked rice ■
3 cups shredded cooked chicken, pork or beef
1 cup shredded mint
3/4 cup coriander (cilantro) leaves
4 kaffir lime leaves, shredded
3 tablespoons lime juice
1 tablespoon caster (superfine) sugar
2 tablespoons fish sauce

Heat a frying pan or wok over high heat. Add the oil, lemongrass, chillies and spring onions and cook for 3 minutes. Place the rice, meat, mint, coriander, lime leaves and lemongrass mixture into a bowl and toss to combine. Combine the lime juice, sugar and fish sauce and pour over the salad. Chill until ready to serve. Serves 4.
■ Use long-grain rice such as jasmine for this recipe.

stirred tomato risotto with mussels

2 tablespoons olive oil
3 leeks, chopped
2 tablespoons lemon thyme leaves
3 1/2–4 cups (28 fl oz–1 3/4 pints) fish or vegetable stock
1 1/2 cups (12 fl oz) tomato purée
2 cups arborio or carnaroli rice
3/4 cup (6 fl oz) white wine
1 tablespoon butter
1 kg (2 lb) mussels, scrubbed
1/2 cup grated parmesan cheese
cracked black pepper and sea salt

Heat a heavy-based frying pan over medium heat. Add the oil, leeks and thyme and cook for 4 minutes or until the leeks are golden. Place the stock and tomato purée in a saucepan and bring to a slow simmer. Add the rice to the leek mixture and cook, stirring, for 2 minutes. Add the hot stock to the rice, 1 cup (8 fl oz) at a time, stirring until each cup of stock is absorbed and the rice is al dente.
While the rice is cooking, place the wine and butter in a frying pan over high heat. Add the mussels, cover and cook for 2 minutes or until the mussels have opened.
To serve, stir parmesan, pepper and salt through the risotto and spoon onto serving plates. Top with the mussels and their pan juices. Serves 4.

stirred tomato risotto with mussels

Persian spiced pilaf with harissa-seared beef

2 cups basmati rice
2¼ cups (18 fl oz) vegetable stock
1 cinnamon stick
3 green cardamom pods, bruised
pinch of saffron threads
harissa-seared beef
8 x 1 cm (½ in) thick slices beef fillet or sirloin
1 tablespoon harissa (chilli paste)
3 spring onions (scallions), shredded

Wash the rice well under cold running water. Place
the rice, stock, cinnamon, cardamom and saffron in a
saucepan over medium heat. Allow to come to the boil,
cover with a tight-fitting lid and reduce the heat to low.
Cook the rice for 12 minutes or until soft. Discard the
cinnamon stick and cardamom pods.
While the rice is cooking, prepare the beef by spreading a
little harissa on each side of the steaks and sprinkle with
the shredded spring onions. Preheat a frying pan over high
heat. Cook the steaks for 2 minutes on each side or until
cooked to your liking.
To serve, place the rice on serving plates and top with the
steak and spring onions. Serve with a little plain yoghurt
mixed with chopped mint if you wish. Serves 4.

sushi sandwiches

2½ cups cooked short-grain rice, cooled ■
2 tablespoons water
2 tablespoons white wine vinegar
1 tablespoon caster (superfine) sugar
2 sheets nori*
8 slices fresh or smoked salmon
1 seedless cucumber, sliced
50g (1½ oz) snowpea (mange tout) sprouts,
    tough stems removed

Combine the rice, water, vinegar and sugar and mix well.
Spread half the rice on one nori sheet to make a base. Top
with the salmon, cucumber and snowpea sprouts. Spread
the remaining rice over the remaining nori sheet. Flip on
top of the filling.
Cut the sandwiches into 4 squares and then in half
diagonally to make small sandwiches. Serve with soy sauce
and wasabi on the side. Serves 4 as a starter or 2 for main.
■ Cook the rice according to the absorption method on
page 36 so that the grains stick together.

crisp rice omelette

2 tablespoons peanut oil
1½ cups cooked rice ■
4 spring onions (scallions), shredded
2 red chillies, seeded and chopped
150g (5 oz) snowpeas (mange tout), shredded
6 eggs, lightly beaten
thick soy or kecap manis* to serve

Preheat the oven to 180°C (350°F). Heat a 20 cm (8 in)
non-stick frying pan over high heat. Add the oil and rice
and cook, stirring, for 5 minutes or until the rice is slightly
crisp. Add the spring onions, chillies and snowpeas and
cook for 2 minutes.
Pour over the eggs and stir for 1 minute. Reduce the heat
to low and cook, without stirring, for 5 minutes. Finish
cooking the omelette in the oven for 3 minutes or until
the omelette has set. To serve, slice into pieces and drizzle
with soy or kecap manis. Serves 4.
■ Jasmine or short-grain rice is best.

baked chicken, lemon and pea risotto

2 tablespoons olive oil
3 chicken breast fillets, quartered
2 leeks, sliced
1 tablespoon shredded lemon zest
2 cups arborio or carnaroli rice
5 cups (2 pints) chicken stock
1½ cups frozen peas ■
2 tablespoons lemon juice
½ cup finely grated parmesan cheese
2 tablespoons chopped mint
cracked black pepper and sea salt

Preheat the oven to 200°C (400°F). Heat a frying pan over
high heat. Add the oil and chicken and cook for 3 minutes
on each side or until well browned. Set aside.
Add the leeks and zest to the pan and cook for 5 minutes
or until the leeks are golden. Place the leek mixture, rice
and stock in a baking dish. Cover tightly with a lid or
aluminium foil and bake for 20 minutes. Add the chicken
and peas to the risotto, cover tightly and bake for a further
20 minutes. The risotto will be quite liquid.
Stir the lemon juice, parmesan, mint, pepper and salt
through the risotto. Stir for 2 minutes to thicken the risotto
and serve. Serves 4.
■ Use 1½ cups of freshly shelled peas if you prefer.

Persian spiced pilaf with harissa-seared beef

crisp rice omelette

sushi sandwiches

baked chicken, lemon and pea risotto

coconut rice with caramelised banana   sweet lemon risotto

coconut rice with caramelised banana

1 cup long or short-grain rice
2 cups (16 fl oz) water
1 cinnamon stick
3/4 cup (6 fl oz) coconut cream
1/3 cup sugar
caramelised banana
4 firm bananas, peeled and halved lengthwise
1/2 cup sugar
1 1/2 teaspoons ground cinnamon

Place the rice in a colander and wash well. Place the rice, water and cinnamon stick in a saucepan over medium to high heat and bring to the boil. Cover tightly and reduce the heat to low and cook for 10 minutes or until the water has been absorbed. Add the coconut cream and sugar, cover the saucepan and place over very low heat for 5 minutes. While the rice is cooking, sprinkle the bananas with the sugar and cinnamon. Preheat a non-stick frying pan over high heat. Cook the bananas for 2 minutes on each side or until the sugar has caramelised.
To serve, place the coconut rice on serving plates and top with the banana slices. Serves 4.

sweet lemon risotto

3 1/2 cups (28 fl oz) milk
6 pieces lemon rind
2 tablespoons butter
1 cup arborio or carnaroli rice
1/3 cup sugar

Preheat the oven to 190°C (375°F). Place the milk, lemon rind and butter in a saucepan over medium heat for 5 minutes or until the milk is hot but not boiling. Place the rice, sugar and milk mixture in a shallow heatproof dish and cover tightly with a lid or aluminium foil. Bake the risotto for 30 minutes.
Remove the risotto from the oven and stir for 2 minutes, then remove the lemon rind. The risotto should be creamy and a little soupy.
To serve, spoon the rice into serving bowls and garnish with the lemon rind if you wish. This makes a great breakfast with yoghurt, or serve it for brunch or dessert with cream. Serves 4–6.

short order

baked vanilla rice peaches

basic fruit and rice custard

cinnamon rice porridge

short order

baked vanilla rice peaches

Combine 1/2 cup cooked short or long-grain rice with 1 tablespoon sugar, 1/4 cup (2 fl oz) cream and 1 teaspoon vanilla extract. Halve and remove the stones from 4 peaches and place in a baking tray, cut side up. Fill the cavities with rice mixture and sprinkle with demerara sugar. Cover with foil and bake in a preheated 180°C (350°F) oven for 20 minutes or until soft. Serve warm.

basic fruit and rice custard

Place cooked fruit such as sweetened rhubarb in the bottom of 6 x 1 cup (8 fl oz) capacity ramekins. Sprinkle each with 1 tablespoon cooked short or long-grain rice. Combine 2 eggs, 2 1/4 cups (18 fl oz) milk and 1/2 cup caster (superfine) sugar and pour over the fruit. Place the ramekins in a baking dish and fill with water to come halfway up the ramekin sides. Bake in an oven preheated to 120°C (250°F) for 45 minutes or until the custards are set.

cinnamon rice porridge

Makes a great breakfast or sweet supper. Combine 1/2 cup short-grain rice with 1 1/2 cups (12 fl oz) water, 1 cup (8 fl oz) milk and 1/2 teaspoon ground cinnamon in a saucepan. Simmer, stirring occasionally, until the rice is very soft and the mixture has a porridge consistency. Spoon into bowls, sprinkle with brown sugar and serve with extra milk.

lemon and basil pilaf

Wash 1 1/2 cups basmati rice and place in a saucepan with 2 cups (16 fl oz) vegetable or chicken stock and 1 tablespoon shredded lemon zest. Cook over medium heat until almost all the stock has been absorbed. Remove from the heat, cover tightly and allow to stand for 5 minutes. Stir through pepper, salt and 1/4 cup chopped basil. Serve with grilled chicken or fish.

gingered rice

Add 2 tablespoons shredded ginger before cooking rice by the absorption method. The rice has a pungent ginger taste and is great to serve with Asian dishes or grilled fish.

parmesan risotto balls

Take a little leftover risotto and shape into a flat pattie. Place a piece of parmesan cheese in the middle and press the risotto over to enclose it. Shallow-fry in hot peanut or olive oil until golden. Serve with drinks or as a meal with salad greens.

rice-stuffed vine leaves

Combine 2 cups cooked rice, 2 tablespoons lemon juice, 1 tablespoon each of chopped parsley and dill, 2 tablespoons pine nuts, pepper and sea salt. Take rinsed pickled vine leaves and place a little of the mixture on each leaf. Roll and fold to enclose the filling. Place the rolls in a baking dish, pour over 1 cup (8 fl oz) vegetable stock and 1 tablespoon olive oil and bake, covered, in a preheated 180°C (350°F) oven for 30 minutes. Cool and serve with drinks.

toasted sesame rice

Heat 2 tablespoons peanut oil in a frying pan over medium heat. Add 2 tablespoons sesame seeds and cook for 1 minute or until golden. Add 4 cups cooked rice to the pan and toss with the sesame seeds until heated through. Stir through sliced spring onions (scallions) and serve.

rice crust pie

Mix 3 cups cooked long-grain rice with 1 egg and 1/2 cup finely grated parmesan cheese. Press into 6 greased 12 cm (5 in) pie tins. Bake in a preheated 180°C (350°F) oven for 10 minutes or until set. Fill the pie shells with a mixture of roast vegetables and cheeses and bake until the filling is hot.

lemon and basil pilaf

gingered rice

parmesan risotto balls

rice-stuffed vine leaves

rice crust pie

toasted sesame rice

noodles

rice
egg
bean thread
wheat
ramen
somen

basics

rice noodles

Made from ground rice and water, these noodles come in different widths, ranging from a thin vermicelli to a wide fettuccine. They need to be soaked or boiled in water until al dente before being combined with other ingredients. These noodles soak up the flavours of a sauce very well and are ideal to use in a stir-fry. Try them in coconut or stock-based soups too.

bean thread noodles

Often called cellophane or glass noodles, these are made from the starch of mung beans and are most commonly sold as very fine strands tied tightly in bundles. Because the bundled noodles are hard to separate when dry, it is best to cut them with a pair of scissors. To cook, simply soak the noodles in boiling water until soft and drain well. They are perfect in coconut-based soups and make a substantial base for a salad.

egg noodles

These are Chinese wheat noodles that have been enriched with egg. They come in varying thicknesses, from vermicelli to fettuccine-sized. You may find egg noodles sold in packets as tight bundles or as long strands. Because they are wheat-based, egg noodles need to be cooked in boiling water until soft before being mixed with other ingredients or added to a soup or stir-fry.

Chinese wheat noodles or ramen

These noodles range from the humble quick-cook variety to the Japanese version – ramen – which is commonly used in soups. Somen, the more delicate Japanese wheat noodle, also falls into this category. All varieties come in thicknesses similar to spaghetti, and they all require the same preparation: first boil in hot water, then add to ingredients or to a soup or stir-fry.

tricks + tips

soup noodles

When serving a noodle soup for more than one person, it is much easier to drain the cooked noodles and place them in the bottom of individual serving bowls, and then pour over the liquid. This way, there is an equal quantity of noodles for each person and a lot less mess.

stir-frying

When stir-frying noodles, you will need to use enough oil (2–3 tablespoons) so that they won't stick together or clump in a gluggy mass. An alternative is to stir-fry the noodles in sauce combinations such as sweet chilli, ginger and soy; or fish sauce, lime juice and brown sugar. Stir-frying the noodles in a sauce also ensures good absorption of the flavours.

soak or boil

Thin noodles such as bean thread and rice varieties only need to be soaked in boiling water until they are cooked and tender. Thicker rice noodles or those containing wheat as their base need to be cooked in a saucepan of boiling water over heat for 3–4 minutes to make them tender.

salad noodles

If you need cool noodles for a salad, after cooking them, rinse under cold water for a few minutes or until they are cool and the surface starch has been washed away.

take the cut

Long strands of noodles are sometimes difficult to eat. A simple solution is to randomly snip the cooked noodles into smaller lengths with a pair of scissors.

honey-seared salmon with coriander noodles   chilli cashew chicken noodles

Asian chicken noodle soup

honey-seared salmon with coriander noodles

550g (18½ oz) salmon fillet
2 tablespoons honey
cracked black pepper
coriander noodles
200g (7 oz) dried somen, Chinese wheat or egg noodles
½ cup coriander (cilantro) leaves
⅓ cup shredded mint leaves
⅓ cup basil leaves, halved
2 zucchini (courgette), shredded
1 tablespoon lime juice
2 tablespoons soy sauce
2 tablespoons honey

To make the coriander noodles, cook the noodles in boiling water for 3–5 minutes or until soft. Drain and rinse under cold running water until cool. Drain again. Combine the noodles with the coriander, mint, basil, zucchini, lime juice, soy and honey.
Cut the salmon into 2 cm (¾ in) wide strips and toss with the honey and pepper. Heat a non-stick frying pan over high heat. Cook the salmon for 1 minute on each side or until the honey is golden.
To serve, place the noodles on serving plates and top with the salmon. Serves 4.

chilli cashew chicken noodles

200g (7 oz) dried thick rice noodles
2 tablespoons peanut oil
2 onions, sliced into wedges
4 large red chillies, seeded and chopped
¼ cup sugar
4 chicken breast fillets, sliced
1 red capsicum (bell pepper), sliced
¾ cup roasted unsalted cashews
2 tablespoons fish sauce*
2 tablespoons soy sauce
2 tablespoons lemon juice
¼ cup coriander (cilantro) leaves

Place the noodles in a saucepan of boiling water and cook for 3 minutes or until tender. Drain.
Heat a wok or deep frying pan over high heat. Add the oil, onions, chillies and sugar and cook for 2 minutes. Remove from the pan and set aside. Add the chicken and cook, stirring, for 4 minutes or until the chicken is golden. Add the capsicum, cashews, fish sauce, soy, lemon juice, onion mixture and noodles to the pan. Cook, stirring, for a further 4 minutes or until heated through. Sprinkle with coriander. Serve with chilli sauce on the side if desired. Serves 4.

Asian chicken noodle soup

150g (5 oz) dried thin egg noodles
6 cups (2 pints 8 fl oz) chicken stock
2 cups (16 fl oz) water
2 star anise
¼ cup (2 fl oz) soy sauce
1 cinnamon stick
3 slices ginger
2 chicken breast fillets
4 spring onions (scallions), shredded

Place the noodles in boiling water and allow to stand for 5 minutes, then drain and set aside.
Place the stock, water, star anise, soy, cinnamon and ginger into a saucepan and cover. Simmer over medium heat for 5 minutes. Add the chicken fillets and cook for 5–7 minutes. Remove and shred the chicken.
Return the chicken to the saucepan with the noodles and spring onions. Cook for 3 minutes or until the noodles are heated through. Serve in deep bowls with spoons and chopsticks. Serves 4.

noodle salad with crisp tofu

150g (5 oz) bean thread or dried thin rice noodles ▪
¼ cup (2 fl oz) peanut oil
375g (12 oz) firm tofu*, thinly shredded
2 carrots, shredded
½ cup chopped roasted peanuts
½ cup coriander (cilantro) leaves
2 cucumbers, sliced lengthwise
dressing
1 tablespoon sesame oil
3 tablespoons soy sauce
1 tablespoon lemon juice

Place the bean thread noodles in a bowl and cover with boiling water. Allow to stand for 5 minutes, then drain.
Heat a frying pan over high heat. Add the oil and tofu and fry for 5 minutes or until crisp. Drain.
To make the dressing, combine the sesame oil, soy and lemon juice.
To serve, toss the noodles with the tofu, carrots, peanuts, coriander and dressing. Place the cucumber on serving plates and top with the salad. Serves 4.
▪ If using rice noodles, cook in boiling water until al dente, then drain.

noodle salad with crisp tofu

shredded chicken and mint noodle salad

200g (7 oz) bean thread or dried thin rice noodles ▪
3 cooked chicken breast fillets, shredded
1 cup shredded mint leaves
100g (3¹/₂ oz) beansprouts or snowpea
   mange tout) sprouts
3 tablespoons sesame seeds
dressing
3 tablespoons fish sauce*
2 tablespoons sugar
3 tablespoons lime juice
1 mild chilli, seeded and chopped

Place the bean thread noodles in a bowl and cover with
boiling water. Allow to stand for 5 minutes, then drain.
Toss the chicken with the noodles, mint, beansprouts
and sesame seeds.
To make the dressing, combine the fish sauce, sugar, lime
juice and chilli.
Pour the dressing over the salad and chill until ready to
serve. Serves 4.
▪ If using rice noodles, cook in boiling water until al dente,
then drain.

lime beef and noodle salad

2 tablespoons peanut oil
750g (1¹/₂ lb) rump or topside steak, sliced
¹/₂ cup (4 fl oz) sweet chilli sauce*
¹/₃ cup (2¹/₂ fl oz) lime juice
8 spring onions (scallions), sliced
6 kaffir lime leaves, shredded
lime wedges to serve
salad
150g (5 oz) thin dried rice noodles
2 Lebanese (seedless) cucumbers, sliced
4 stalks celery, finely sliced
100g (3¹/₂ oz) lettuce leaves

Heat the oil in a frying pan or wok over high heat. Add
the beef in 2 batches and cook for 5 minutes or until
well sealed. Set aside. Add the chilli sauce, lime juice,
spring onions and lime leaves to the pan and cook for
4 minutes, then pour over the beef.
To make the salad, place the noodles in a saucepan of
boiling water and cook for 2 minutes or until tender. Drain
and rinse under cold water. Combine the noodles with the
cucumber, celery and lettuce and place on serving plates.
Top with the beef mixture and serve with lime wedges.
Serves 4.

shredded chicken and mint noodle salad

lime beef and noodle salad

squid and noodle salad

8 medium-sized squid hoods, scored ▪
4 zucchini (courgette), sliced lengthwise
1/4 cup (2 fl oz) sweet chilli sauce*
1 tablespoon lime juice
1 tablespoon peanut oil
noodle salad
200g (7 oz) dried thin rice noodles
3 tablespoons toasted sesame seeds
2 teaspoons sesame oil
2 tablespoons soy sauce
2 tablespoons shredded basil leaves
2 tablespoons lime juice, extra

Rinse the squid and quarter. Place in a bowl with the zucchini, chilli sauce, lime juice and peanut oil and refrigerate for 20 minutes.
Heat a barbecue or frying pan over high heat. Add the squid and zucchini, a few pieces at a time, and cook until golden and tender.
Place the noodles in a bowl of boiling water and allow to stand for 5 minutes. Drain.
Toss the noodles with the sesame seeds, sesame oil, soy, basil and lime juice. Pile the noodles onto serving plates and top with the squid and zucchini. Serve with lime wedges if desired. Serves 4.
▪ To score the squid, run the point of a sharp knife over the surface so that it cuts the flesh about halfway through.

bok choy and noodle stir-fry

250g (8 oz) dried somen or Chinese wheat noodles
2 tablespoons peanut oil
2 tablespoons shredded ginger
2 cloves garlic, sliced
1 large red chilli, sliced
8 heads bok choy, quartered lengthwise
12 fresh shiitake mushrooms, halved
1 cup (8 fl oz) chicken stock
2 tablespoons soy sauce

Place the noodles in a saucepan of boiling water and cook for 3 minutes or until soft. Drain.
Heat the oil in a deep frying pan or wok. Add the ginger, garlic and chilli and cook for 1 minute. Add the bok choy and mushrooms and cook for 2 minutes. Add the chicken stock and soy and allow to cook for a further 4 minutes or until the bok choy is soft.
To serve, place the noodles in a bowl and top with the bok choy mixture. Serves 4.

noodles and fish in chilli broth

200g (7 oz) dried egg noodles
5 cups (2 pints) vegetable or fish stock
2 tablespoons soy sauce
3 large mild chillies, seeded and sliced
4 kaffir lime leaves, shredded
1 tablespoon shredded ginger
600g (20 oz) firm fish such as cod or salmon, cubed
fried spring onions (scallions) to serve

Place the noodles in a saucepan of boiling water and cook for 3 minutes or until tender. Drain. Place the stock, soy, chillies, lime leaves and ginger in a saucepan over medium heat and simmer for 5 minutes. Add the fish and cook for 1 minute or until tender.
To serve, pile the noodles in serving bowls. Top with the fish and ladle over the stock. Serve topped with the fried spring onions. Serves 4.

stir-fried noodles with crispy chicken

200g (7 oz) dried Chinese wheat noodles
2 tablespoons peanut oil
2 large red chillies, seeded and chopped
2 tablespoons shredded ginger
600g (20 oz) gai larn or Asian greens, sliced
3 tablespoons hoisin sauce*
1/4 cup (2 fl oz) soy sauce
1 tablespoon sugar
crispy chicken
4 chicken breast fillets, sliced
2 egg whites, lightly whisked
1 cup rice flour
2 teaspoons Chinese five-spice powder*
1 teaspoon salt
extra peanut oil to shallow-fry

Place the noodles in a saucepan of boiling water and cook for 3 minutes or until soft. Drain and set aside.
Heat the oil in a frying pan or wok over high heat. Add the chillies and ginger and cook for 2 minutes. Add the gai larn, hoisin sauce, soy and sugar and cook for 4 minutes or until the vegetables are tender. Toss through the noodles.
To make the crispy chicken, dip the chicken pieces into the egg white, then toss in the combined rice flour, Chinese five-spice powder and salt. Heat enough oil in a saucepan to shallow-fry the chicken and cook a few pieces at a time until golden.
To serve, place the noodle mixture on serving plates and top with the crispy chicken. Serves 4.

squid and noodle salad

noodles and fish in chilli broth

bok choy and noodle stir-fry

stir-fried noodles with crispy chicken

short order

noodle cakes

pork noodle salad

seared scallops on noodles

short order

noodle cakes

Place piles of cooked rice noodles in a frying pan with 2 cm (3/4 in) hot peanut oil. Flatten the noodles with a spatula to form a flat cake. Cook for 2 minutes on each side or until crisp. Drain on absorbent paper and top with coriander (cilantro) leaves and shredded cooked chicken. Serve as an appetiser or with drinks. You can also use the noodle cakes as you would a small cracker.

pork noodle salad

Cook 200g (7 oz) thick rice noodles until tender. Drain and cool. Heat 1 tablespoon peanut oil in a frying pan. Add 2 tablespoons shredded ginger and 500g (1 lb) minced (ground) pork and cook for 6 minutes. Add 1/4 cup (2 fl oz) hoisin sauce and 1/2 cup (4 fl oz) chicken stock and cook for 2 minutes. Cool. Toss the pork mixture, 1/2 cup coriander (cilantro) leaves and 3/4 cup shredded basil through the noodles and serve with lemon wedges.

seared scallops on noodles

Sear 12 scallops in a hot pan for 20 seconds on each side. Place a pile of cooked somen or wheat noodles in a bowl. Pour over hot chicken or fish stock and sprinkle with shredded spring onions (scallions). Top with the scallops and serve.

spicy soup

Cook 200g (7 oz) egg noodles until al dente, then drain. Place 1–2 tablespoons red or green curry paste in a saucepan over medium to high heat and cook for 2 minutes. Add 3 cups (24 fl oz) chicken stock and 2 cups (16 fl oz) coconut cream and simmer for 4 minutes. Add 2 sliced chicken breast fillets and 150g (5 oz) green beans, halved, and cook for 4 minutes. Add noodles and cook until heated through. Serve in bowls with spoons and chopsticks.

crispy fried noodles

Place uncooked bean thread noodles in hot peanut oil, a small bunch at a time. They will swell and become crisp in seconds. Drain on absorbent paper. Use in a salad or to sprinkle over stir-fried dishes.

Chinatown pork and noodles

Purchase 500g (1 lb) Chinese barbecue pork fillet from a Chinese barbecue shop. Cut pork into slices. Cook 200g (7 oz) thick rice or egg noodles until tender, then drain. Stir-fry chopped Chinese greens such as bok choy, 1 tablespoon soy sauce and 1 cup (8 fl oz) chicken stock with the noodles. Add the pork and toss until hot, then serve.

stir-fried prawns and noodles

Stir-fry 1 chopped red chilli and 2 cloves sliced garlic in 2 tablespoons peanut oil for 1 minute. Add 500g (1 lb) shelled raw prawns (shrimp) and cook for 3 minutes or until pink. Add 200g (7 oz) cooked egg noodles, 3 shredded bok choy, 2 tablespoons soy sauce and 2 tablespoons sweet chilli sauce. Cook until heated through.

simple snack

For a snack for 1 person, cook 50g (1 1/2 oz) rice noodles until soft. Place the noodles in a bowl and top with 1/2 teaspoon sesame oil, 1 tablespoon soy sauce and 1 tablespoon sweet chilli sauce. Serve warm with shredded spring onions (scallions) if desired.

chilli side dish

For a spicy noodle side dish, cook 200g (7 oz) rice noodles until tender, then drain. Heat a little peanut oil in a frying pan over high heat. Add 3 chopped small red chillies, 2 tablespoons shredded ginger, 2 cloves sliced garlic and cracked black pepper. Cook for 2 minutes, then add the noodles. Toss with small basil leaves.

spicy soup

crispy fried noodles

Chinatown pork and noodles

simple snack

stir-fried prawns and noodles

chilli side dish

grains + lentils

polenta
canned cannellini beans

canned chickpeas
couscous
red lentils
du puy lentils.

basics

polenta

A fine, dry cornmeal that, when cooked with water, milk and butter, forms a thick, creamy paste. I use the 'instant' or quick-cook variety for speed and convenience. You can serve polenta wherever you would have mashed potato. Or allow it to set in a shallow cake tin, cut into small pieces and grill until golden. Combine polenta with simple flavours such as parmesan, pepper and spinach.

canned cannellini beans and chickpeas

Cannellini beans are a white Italian kidney bean. Chickpeas (garbanzo) have a firmer texture and nutty flavour. Both are available in dry and canned forms. Canned beans make a fantastic instant base for a simple meal, salad, side dish or starter. Drain and rinse the beans before using them, and add at the end of cooking so that they are warmed through but retain their shape and texture.

couscous

Made from semolina and wheat that has been rubbed
together, couscous grains vary in size from fine to medium
to coarse. Cook medium or fine-grained couscous by
placing it in hot stock or water and allowing the grains
to 'drink up' the liquid. Couscous has a mild, earthy
taste and is an ideal base for salads, side dishes or spicy
Middle Eastern dishes.

lentils – red and du puy

Red lentils, which are actually bright orange in colour,
take just 5–7 minutes to cook in boiling water. Their spicy
flavour adds texture, volume and interest to salads and
soups. The du puy lentil, originally from France, is a
small, deep green variety with a nutty and earthy flavour.
It is considered the finest quality lentil and complements
rich meat dishes well.

tricks + tips

enhance the flavour

Some foods, such as mashed potato, grilled steak, tomatoes and especially polenta, need added salt to enhance their flavour. I always use a generous amount of sea salt when cooking polenta. You can also add salty ingredients such as parmesan cheese or olives.

traditional couscous

Couscous is traditionally steamed in a *couscoussière* over a simmering well-spiced dish of meat or vegetables in a stock. As it steams and fluffs up, the couscous absorbs the flavours. If you do not have the time, you can use this quick and easy method. Place 1 cup couscous in a bowl and pour over 1 1/4 cups (10 fl oz) boiling stock or water. Cover and allow to stand until the liquid is absorbed. Stir with a fork and add a little butter, pepper and sea salt.

rinse your beans

Although off-putting to some, the liquid in a can of beans is just a mixture of the starch from the beans and the water they were cooked in (they're actually pressure-cooked in the can). All you need to do is drain the beans, transfer to a sieve or colander, and rinse away the starch under cold running water.

quick versus slow

If you have the time, strength and energy to stir the very thick slow-cook polenta for 40 minutes so that it doesn't have the texture of sand, then, by all means, go ahead. For those of us with less time, there is an instant or quick-cook variety which is ready in about 5 minutes and has the same finished qualities as the slow-cook grains. The quick-cook variety can be used to make soft polenta or to set and make grilled polenta dishes.

lentil and goat's cheese tarts

lamb shanks with du puy lentils

chickpea and roast pumpkin soup

lentil and goat's cheese tarts

150g (5 oz) du puy lentils
6 sheets filo pastry
50g (1 1/2 oz) butter, melted
500g (1 lb) ricotta
4 eggs
1 1/2 cups (12 fl oz) milk
1/4 cup chopped flat-leaf parsley
cracked black pepper and sea salt
120g (4 oz) goat's cheese, sliced ■

Place the lentils in a saucepan of boiling water and cook for 15 minutes or until tender. Drain and set aside. Preheat the oven to 160°C (325°F). Cut the pastry sheets in half to make squares. Lightly brush the pastry squares with the butter and make piles of 3 sheets each. Line 4 greased 1 cup (8 fl oz) capacity pie dishes with the pastry, folding to fit the edges in the dishes.
To make the filling, mix the ricotta, eggs and milk in a food processor until smooth. Place in a bowl and stir through the cooked lentils, parsley, pepper and salt. Pour the mixture into the pastry shells and top with the goat's cheese. Bake for 30 minutes or until the filling is set. Serve warm. Serves 4.
■ You can also use blue cheese or aged cheddar.

lamb shanks with du puy lentils

8 lamb shanks, bones trimmed ■
2 x 400g (14 oz) cans whole peeled tomatoes
4 cups (2 pints) beef stock
2 tablespoons brown sugar
2 tablespoons oregano leaves
2 cups du puy lentils

Preheat the oven to 200°C (400°F). Place the lamb shanks, tomatoes, stock, sugar and oregano in a large baking dish and cover tightly. Bake for 45 minutes, then turn the shanks, add the lentils and bake, covered, for a further 45 minutes or until the lamb is soft.
To serve, spoon the lentils and shanks onto serving plates and top with the pan juices. Serve with creamy mashed potato if you wish. Serves 4.
■ Ask your butcher to trim both ends of the shank bones for you.

chickpea and roast pumpkin soup

2 kg (4 lb) pumpkin
6 cups (2 1/2 pints) vegetable or chicken stock
1 tablespoon oil
2 onions, finely chopped
1 teaspoon ground cumin
2 tablespoons Dijon mustard
2 tablespoons honey
1 x 400g (14 oz) can chickpeas, drained and rinsed
1/2 cup shredded basil

Preheat the oven to 200°C (400°F). Cut the pumpkin into large wedges, leaving the skin on. Place the wedges in a baking dish and bake for 40 minutes or until soft and golden. In two batches, scrape the flesh into a food processor with 1 1/2 cups (12 fl oz) of the stock and blend until smooth. Heat a saucepan over medium to high heat. Add the oil, onions and cumin and cook for 4 minutes or until soft. Add the mustard, honey, the remaining stock and the pumpkin purée and simmer for 5 minutes. Stir through the chickpeas and basil and cook for a further 5 minutes. Serve with grilled bread. Serves 4.

spicy coconut and lentil soup

2 teaspoons peanut oil
1–2 tablespoons red curry paste
4 cups (2 pints) vegetable or chicken stock
2 cups (16 fl oz) coconut cream
4 kaffir lime leaves, shredded
1 cup red lentils
100g (3 1/2 oz) button mushrooms, halved
125g (4 oz) fresh or 1 x 400g (14 oz) can
  baby corn, drained and halved
80g (2 1/2 oz) snowpeas (mange tout), halved
1 tablespoon sugar

Place the oil and curry paste in a saucepan over medium to low heat and cook for 2 minutes. Add the stock, coconut cream, lime leaves and lentils to the pan and cook for 10 minutes, stirring occasionally. Add the mushrooms, corn, snowpeas and sugar to the soup and simmer for 3 minutes or until the snowpeas are tender. To serve, ladle the soup into bowls and serve with grilled flatbread. Serves 4.

spicy coconut and lentil soup

beef and caramelised onion couscous salad

750g (1¹/2 lb) beef fillet or thick rump steak, trimmed
1 tablespoon olive oil
cracked black pepper
200g (7 oz) baby English spinach leaves
Dijon mustard to serve
onion couscous
2 tablespoons olive oil
4 onions, sliced
2 cups couscous
2¹/2 cups (1 pint) hot chicken or beef stock
2 tablespoons Dijon mustard
2 tablespoons olive oil, extra
1 tablespoon lemon juice
cracked black pepper and sea salt

Brush the beef with the oil, then sprinkle well with pepper. Heat a non-stick frying pan or barbecue over medium to high heat. Cook the beef for 4 minutes on each side or until cooked to your liking. Set aside and cover.
To make the onion couscous, heat a frying pan over medium heat. Add the oil and onions and cook, stirring occasionally, for 8–10 minutes or until the onions are soft and golden. Place the couscous in a bowl and pour over the hot stock. Cover and allow to stand for 5 minutes or until all the stock has been absorbed.
Combine the mustard, extra oil, lemon juice, pepper and salt and toss with the couscous and the onions. To serve, place the spinach leaves on plates and top with the couscous. Slice the beef and place on top. Serve with extra mustard on the side. Serves 4.

spinach polenta with balsamic tomatoes

4 ripe tomatoes, halved
2 tablespoons olive oil
3 tablespoons balsamic vinegar
3 tablespoons caster (superfine) sugar
3 tablespoons oregano leaves
polenta
2 cups (16 fl oz) hot water
2 cups (16 fl oz) milk
1 cup quick-cook polenta
¹/2 cup grated parmesan cheese
375g (12 oz) English spinach, stems removed ▪
60g (2 oz) butter
cracked black pepper and sea salt

Preheat the oven to 200°C (400°F). Place the tomatoes, cut side down, in an ovenproof ceramic dish. Combine the oil, balsamic, sugar and oregano and pour over the tomatoes. Bake for 20 minutes or until the tomatoes are soft.
Make the polenta while the tomatoes are roasting. Place the water and milk in a saucepan over medium to high heat and bring to the boil. Slowly whisk in the polenta. Reduce the heat to medium-low and cook the polenta, stirring, for 3–5 minutes. Stir through the parmesan, spinach, butter, pepper and salt.
To serve, spoon the polenta onto serving plates. Top with the tomatoes and the pan juices. Finish with extra parmesan and serve. Serves 4.
▪ You can use a 250g (8 oz) packet of frozen English spinach leaves (not chopped) instead of the fresh. Simply defrost and squeeze out any excess moisture.

beef and caramelised onion couscous salad

spinach polenta with balsamic tomatoes

garlic chickpeas with cumin-fried fish

3 tablespoons olive oil
3 leeks, shredded
1 tablespoon shredded lemon zest
3 cloves garlic, sliced
2 x 400g (14 oz) cans chickpeas, drained and rinsed
1/4 cup chopped flat-leaf parsley
cumin-fried fish
1 tablespoon butter
1 tablespoon olive oil
1 tablespoon ground cumin
1 small red chilli, seeded and chopped
4 x 200g (7 oz) firm white-fleshed fish, cut into pieces

Heat a frying pan over medium heat. Cook the oil, leeks
and lemon zest, stirring occasionally, for 8 minutes or until
the leeks are golden and a little crisp. Add the garlic and
cook for 1 minute. Add the chickpeas and cook for
5 minutes or until heated through. Stir through the parsley.
To cook the fish, heat a frying pan over medium heat.
Add the butter, olive oil, cumin and chilli and cook for
3 minutes. Add the fish to the pan and cook for
2–3 minutes on each side or until just cooked through.
Place the chickpeas on serving plates, place the fish
on the side and serve with a lime wedge. Serves 4.

baked couscous with lemon and parsley chicken

2 chicken breast fillets
2 cups couscous
2 1/2 cups (1 pint) chicken stock
1 tablespoon olive oil
cracked black pepper and sea salt
1 tablespoon grated lemon zest
1/4 cup chopped flat-leaf parsley
2 tablespoons salted capers, rinsed and chopped
1/2 cup black olives

Preheat the oven to 200°C (400°F). Heat a little oil in
a frying pan and cook the chicken for 2 minutes on each
side or until golden.
Place the couscous in the base of a medium-sized baking
dish. Pour over the stock, oil, pepper and salt. Place the
chicken on top of the couscous. Combine the lemon zest,
parsley and capers and sprinkle over the chicken. Add the
olives and cover the dish with a lid or aluminium foil. Bake
for 20 minutes or until the chicken is cooked through.
To serve, fluff the couscous with a fork and spoon onto
serving plates. Top with the chicken. Serve with lemon
wedges and rocket (arugula) leaves. Serves 2.

cannellini and fresh tomato broth

6 large ripe tomatoes, quartered ■
4 cups (1 3/4 pints) chicken or vegetable stock
1 x 400g (14 oz) can cannellini beans, drained and rinsed
sea salt and cracked black pepper
2 tablespoons chopped oregano
grilled bread to serve

Place the tomatoes and half the stock in a blender and
blend until smooth. Pour the mixture through a sieve and
place in a saucepan with the remaining stock over medium
heat. Allow the soup to come to the boil and simmer for
8 minutes, then add the cannellini beans, salt, pepper
and oregano. Simmer for 2 minutes and serve in bowls
with grilled bread that has been drizzled with a little
olive oil. Serves 4.
■ Using really ripe tomatoes will give this soup a wonderful
sweet flavour. If perfect tomatoes are not available, you
may need to add a pinch of sugar to help boost the flavour.

creamy polenta with caramelised fennel

85g (2 1/2 oz) butter
2 medium-sized fennel, trimmed and quartered
1 cup (8 fl oz) chicken stock
1/2 cup brown sugar
1/3 cup (2 1/2 fl oz) white wine vinegar
8 sprigs thyme
160g (5 1/2 oz) blue cheese, sliced
polenta
2 cups (16 fl oz) hot water
2 cups (16 fl oz) milk
1 cup quick-cook polenta
60g (2 oz) butter
cracked black pepper and sea salt

Place the butter in a deep frying pan over medium heat.
Add the fennel and cook for 4 minutes on each side or
until well browned. Add the stock, sugar, vinegar and
thyme to the pan and cover and cook for 8 minutes or
until the fennel is soft and golden. Remove the fennel
from the pan and keep warm.
Bring the pan juices to the boil and reduce by half.
While the sauce is simmering, make the polenta. Place the
water and milk in a saucepan over medium to high heat
and bring to the boil. Slowly whisk in the polenta. Reduce
the heat to medium-low and cook the polenta, stirring, for
3–5 minutes. Stir through the butter, pepper and salt.
To serve, place a large spoonful of polenta on each serving
plate. Top with a slice of blue cheese, then the fennel and
the pan juices. Serves 4.

garlic chickpeas with cumin-fried fish

cannellini and fresh tomato broth

baked couscous with lemon and parsley chicken

creamy polenta with caramelised fennel

short order

couscous stuffing

grilled polenta

lentil and potato mash

short order

couscous stuffing

To make a simple stuffing, combine 1 cup couscous with 1 1/4 cups (10 fl oz) boiling stock, cover and stand until all the stock is absorbed. Mix with chopped fresh herbs, 2 chopped and browned onions or leeks, and cracked black pepper and sea salt. Use as a stuffing for meats or whole fish.

grilled polenta

A great side dish or top with blue cheese and rocket (arugula) leaves to make a simple meal. Make a quantity of soft polenta (below). After cooking, spread out in an oiled 20 cm x 30 cm (8 in x 12 in) tray and refrigerate until set. Remove the polenta from the tray and cut into pieces. Brush with oil and grill (broil) or cook in a hot frying pan for 2–3 minutes on each side or until golden.

lentil and potato mash

Mash potatoes with a little warm milk, butter and salt. Stir through some cooked du puy lentils and serve as a winter side dish. Allow 1 large potato and 2 tablespoons raw lentils per person.

soft polenta

Serve this as you would mashed potato. Heat 2 cups (16 fl oz) milk and 2 cups (16 fl oz) water over medium heat until hot. Whisk in 1 cup quick-cook polenta and cook, stirring, for 5 minutes or until the polenta grains are soft. Stir through plenty of butter, cracked black pepper and sea salt. Top with parmesan or goat's cheese, butter, cracked black pepper and sea salt.

marinated chickpea salad

Combine 2 x 400g (14 oz) cans drained chickpeas with 1/3 cup (2 1/2 fl oz) lemon juice, 1 crushed garlic clove, 1/2 cup chopped flat-leaf parsley, 2 tablespoons olive oil, 1/3 cup shaved parmesan cheese, cracked black pepper and sea salt. Allow to marinate for at least 30 minutes before serving with baby spinach leaves as a salad.

lentil purée

This spicy dip is delicious as part of a mezze plate or with grilled flatbread. In a saucepan, place 1 cup red lentils and 1 1/2 cups (12 fl oz) water and boil for 2 minutes. Cover and allow to stand for 12 minutes. Place the lentils in a food processor with 1/3 cup (2 1/2 fl oz) olive oil, 1/4 cup (2 fl oz) lemon juice, 1 crushed garlic clove, 1 teaspoon ground cumin and sea salt. Process until smooth.

couscous salad

Cook 2 cups couscous in 2 1/2 cups (1 pint) hot chicken stock following the directions on page 72. Toss the warm couscous with 700g (23 oz) roasted diced pumpkin or sweet potato and 200g (7 oz) blanched snowpeas (mange tout). Combine 3 tablespoons olive oil, 1/2 teaspoon harissa or chilli paste, 1/4 cup chopped mint, 1/4 cup lemon juice and 1 tablespoon honey. Pour the dressing over the couscous, toss and serve.

chickpea and goat's cheese felafel

Place 2 x 400g (14 oz) cans drained chickpeas, 1/2 finely chopped red onion, 1 1/2 cups fresh breadcrumbs, 1/2 cup each of coriander (cilantro) leaves, mint leaves and flat-leaf parsley and 2 teaspoons ground cumin in a food processor and process until the mixture is finely chopped. Shape into rounded patties with a small piece of goat's cheese inside, then refrigerate for 30 minutes. Shallow-fry in hot peanut oil until golden and drain on absorbent paper. Serve with a squeeze of lemon with drinks.

cannellini bean salad

Combine 2 x 400g (14 oz) cans drained cannellini beans, 200g (7 oz) blanched and halved green beans, 200g (7 oz) halved cherry tomatoes, 1 teaspoon paprika, 1/2 cup chopped mint, 1/2 cup chopped flat-leaf parsley, 2 tablespoons olive oil, 1/4 cup (2 fl oz) lemon juice, cracked black pepper and sea salt. Serve with grilled flatbread.

soft polenta

marinated chickpea salad

lentil purée

couscous salad

chickpea and goat's cheese felafel

cannellini bean salad

canned tomatoes
canned tuna
salted capers

mediterranean

balsamic vinegar
olive oil
olives

basics

canned tomatoes and tuna

A convenient must-have for every pantry. With these two products on hand, many a quick meal can be achieved. Purchase whole peeled tomatoes in tomato juice (not crushed tomatoes) to be assured of the quality.
For maximum flavour, choose canned tuna packed in olive oil rather than brine. You may need to try a few different brands before you find a favourite.

salted capers

Capers are the small, deep green flower buds of the caper bush. They can be purchased packed either in a brine or dry in salt. I find that capers packed in salt are superior in taste and texture to their briny counterparts. Rinse capers well before using. They are a great addition to pasta sauces and also go well with fish and meats. Choose smaller, firmer capers over the larger variety.

balsamic vinegar

This dark and mellow vinegar from Italy has a very rounded and rich flavour not found in other types. While tart like other vinegars, it has a less astringent taste and more of a rich, red wine flavour. Like some good wines, the older a balsamic vinegar is, the better it is, so buy a bottle that has a few years behind it. An aged vinegar will have a thicker consistency and smoother taste.

olive oil and olives

The taste of a great olive oil is a magical thing, and if you've only ever used the mass-produced variety, you haven't lived. A good-quality cold-pressed or first-pressed extra virgin olive oil is indispensable. As are black or green olives, which can add extra complexity to many dishes. Choose firm olives with good colour and a fruity taste.

tricks + tips

the balsamic age

Excellent to use in salad dressings, this full-bodied Italian vinegar is also wonderful with meat, chicken and game. Although you can buy expensive, well-aged balsamic vinegars from five to 25 years old (some so exquisite, they can be drunk as an aperitif), for everyday cooking, a quality brand with a few years' age will be fine.

do those olives need soaking?

Before adding olives, whether black or green, to a dish, check how salty they are. If they taste more salty than fruity, you can soak them in cold water to dilute the salt. If they are really salty, you may need to change the water a few times.

cooked or cold

A fruity green olive oil that is low in acid is perfect for serving with crusty bread or using in salad dressings where the pure taste and quality of the oil is important. For cooking, where the pure flavour is not so important, use a less expensive extra virgin olive oil. Like all fresh products, olive oil is better when just pressed. Some olive oil bottles give the date of pressing or the year of the harvest. If you can, always buy a young, fresh olive oil.

the salt caper

I didn't like capers until I tasted a salted one. The texture of salted capers is much firmer than those packed in brine, which are often soft and soggy and taste strongly of the brine solution. Salted capers have a zingy flavour but are also a little salty, like an olive. Salted capers need to be thoroughly rinsed before use. If you still find them salty, soak them in cold water for a few minutes.

gremolata seared chicken

parmesan-crusted veal cutlets

green olive baked chicken

gremolata seared chicken

2 tablespoons olive oil
4 chicken breast fillets
gremolata
1/2 cup finely chopped flat-leaf parsley
1 tablespoon salted capers, rinsed and chopped
1 tablespoon finely grated lemon zest
cracked black pepper

To make the gremolata, combine the parsley, capers, lemon zest and enough pepper to taste. Sprinkle the chicken with the gremolata mixture.
Heat the oil in a non-stick frying pan over medium to low heat. Add the chicken and cook for 5 minutes on each side or until cooked through. Serve with salt-roasted potatoes and steamed green beans. Serves 4.

parmesan-crusted veal cutlets

4 thick veal cutlets, trimmed
2 egg whites, lightly beaten
1 1/2 cups finely grated parmesan cheese ■
cracked black pepper
tomato and basil sauce
2 teaspoons olive oil
1 onion, chopped
2 x 400g (14 oz) cans whole peeled tomatoes
2 tablespoons brown sugar
1/2 cup roughly chopped basil leaves
cracked black pepper and sea salt

To make the tomato and basil sauce, heat a frying pan over medium heat. Add the oil and onion and cook for 5 minutes or until soft. Add the tomatoes and sugar, keeping the tomatoes whole. Simmer for 10 minutes, turning the tomatoes occasionally, or until the sauce has reduced. Carefully stir through the basil, pepper and salt. While the sauce is cooking, gently dip the cutlets into the egg whites and drain off any excess. Combine the parmesan and some pepper and transfer to a flat plate. Firmly press both sides of the cutlet into the parmesan. Heat a non-stick frying pan over medium heat. Add the cutlets and cook for 4 minutes on each side or until just golden and cooked to your liking. Place some tomato and basil sauce on each plate and top with a cutlet. Serve with baked fennel if desired. Serves 4.
■ You will get better results if you use a good-quality parmesan cheese. The secret to this recipe is not to turn the veal until the parmesan is golden and cooked.

green olive baked chicken

3/4 cup pitted green olives, halved
1.6 kg (3.2 lb) whole chicken
4 cloves garlic, peeled and halved
1/2 cup chopped flat-leaf parsley
2 tablespoons grated lemon zest
250g (8 oz) cherry tomatoes
cracked black pepper and sea salt
2 tablespoons olive oil

Preheat the oven to 200°C (400°F). Soak the olives in cold water for 5 minutes to remove the excess salt. Drain. Divide the chicken into 8 pieces or ask your butcher to do so. Place the chicken in a baking dish, skin side up, and put a piece of garlic under each chicken portion. Combine the olives, parsley, lemon zest, tomatoes, pepper, salt and olive oil and spoon over the chicken.
Bake for 45–55 minutes or until the chicken is golden and cooked through. Place on serving plates and serve drizzled with the pan juices. Serves 4.

lamb cutlets with vine leaves and lemon

12 lamb cutlets
cracked black pepper and sea salt
1 tablespoon olive oil
1 tablespoon shredded lemon zest
1 tablespoon oregano leaves
2 tablespoons olive oil, extra
4 small vine leaves ■

Trim the cutlets of excess fat and sprinkle both sides with a little pepper and salt. Heat a large frying pan over medium to high heat. Add the oil, lemon zest and oregano and cook for 30 seconds. Add the lamb cutlets and cook for 3 minutes on each side or until cooked to your liking. Remove and set aside.
Heat the extra oil in the frying pan and cook the vine leaves for 2 minutes on each side or until crisp.
Serve the lamb cutlets with mashed potato that has been drizzled with olive oil and sprinkled with sea salt, and place a vine leaf on the side. Serves 4.
■ Use vine leaves packed in brine that have been rinsed or fresh vine leaves that have been softened in a little boiling water. Dry well before frying.

lamb cutlets with vine leaves and lemon

tomato and basil poached fish

1 tablespoon olive oil
2 onions, sliced
2 cloves garlic, sliced
6 new baby potatoes, thinly sliced
1/2 cup (4 fl oz) vegetable or fish stock
2 x 400g (14 oz) cans whole peeled tomatoes
cracked black pepper and sea salt
2 x 200g (7 oz) firm white-fleshed fish fillets
1/3 cup chopped basil

Heat a deep frying pan over medium heat. Add the oil,
onions and garlic and cook for 4 minutes or until the
onions are soft. Add the potatoes, stock and tomatoes,
cover and cook for 5 minutes.
Add some pepper and salt to the pan and stir to break
up the tomatoes slightly. Cook, uncovered, for 4 minutes
or until the mixture has reduced and thickened slightly.
Place the fish on top of the tomato mixture in the pan
and cook for 2–3 minutes on each side or until the fish
is cooked to your liking.
To serve, stir through the basil and place the fish and
tomato sauce on serving plates. Top with fried capers
(page 106) if you wish. Serves 2.

onion, anchovy and olive tart

5 brown onions, sliced
3 tablespoons olive oil
2 tablespoons balsamic vinegar
1 tablespoon brown sugar
375g (12 oz) ready-prepared puff pastry
1/4 cup finely grated parmesan cheese
9 anchovy fillets, drained
1/4 cup black olives, halved
2 tablespoons oregano leaves
salad greens to serve

Preheat the oven to 200°C (400°F). Place the onions and
oil in a frying pan over medium heat. Cook, stirring, for
10 minutes or until the onions are soft and golden. Add
the balsamic and sugar and cook for 2 minutes, then set
aside to cool.
Roll out the pastry on a lightly floured surface until 4 mm
(1/8 in) thick. Trim the pastry to a roughly rectangular
shape and place on a lined baking tray. Top the pastry
with the parmesan, leaving a 2 cm (3/4 in) border. Top with
the onions, anchovies, olives and oregano. Bake for 20–25
minutes or until the tart is golden and puffed. Serve warm
in slices with a simple green salad. Serves 4–6.

tomato and basil poached fish

onion, anchovy and olive tart

balsamic lamb salad

pea and tuna tart

balsamic and tomato roast chicken

tuna and grilled vegetable salad

98

balsamic lamb salad

650g (21 oz) boneless lamb loin or fillet
1/2 cup (4 fl oz) balsamic vinegar
1/2 cup (4 fl oz) orange juice
2 tablespoons sugar
2 tablespoons oregano leaves
8 small waxy potatoes, halved
125g (4 oz) salad leaves

Trim the lamb and place in a shallow dish.
Combine the balsamic, orange juice, sugar and oregano
and pour over the lamb. Allow the lamb to marinate for
10 minutes on each side.
While the lamb is marinating, boil or steam the potatoes
until soft, then rinse under cold water to cool.
Heat a frying pan over high heat. Remove the lamb
from the marinade and cook the meat in the pan for
3–4 minutes on each side. Place on a plate and cover
to keep warm. Add the marinade to the pan and cook
for 2 minutes.
To serve, place the salad greens and potatoes on serving
plates. Slice the lamb, place on the salad and spoon over
the warm pan juices. Serves 4.

balsamic and tomato roast chicken

4 thick slices eggplant (aubergine), cut lengthwise
4 chicken breast fillets
1 x 400g (14 oz) can whole peeled tomatoes,
    drained and quartered
2 tablespoons salted capers, rinsed
1/4 cup (2 fl oz) balsamic vinegar
1 tablespoon olive oil
2 tablespoons brown sugar
1/4 cup whole basil leaves
cracked black pepper

Preheat the oven to 200°C (400°F). Place the eggplant
in the bottom of a baking dish and top each slice with
a chicken breast. Combine the tomatoes, capers, balsamic,
oil and sugar and spread over the chicken breast. Bake
for 20–25 minutes or until the chicken is cooked through.
Sprinkle with the basil leaves and pepper and serve with a
rocket (arugula) salad. Serves 4.

pea and tuna tart

350g (11 1/2 oz) shortcrust pastry*
150g (5 oz) fresh or frozen peas ■
1 1/2 cups (12 fl oz) cream
3 eggs
1/2 cup finely grated parmesan cheese
1/4 cup finely chopped mint
1 tablespoon Dijon mustard
1 x 185g (6 oz) can tuna, drained

Preheat the oven to 190°C (375°F). Roll out the pastry on
a lightly floured surface until 3 mm (1/8 in) thick. Place the
pastry in a 22 cm (9 in) tart tin with a removable base or
a ring on a baking tray. Prick the pastry with a fork and
line with baking paper. Fill the tart with baking weights
or rice and bake for 7 minutes. Remove the weights and
paper and bake for a further 7 minutes or until the pastry
is a light golden colour.
To make the filling, place the fresh peas in a saucepan
of boiling water and cook for 4 minutes or until just soft.
Drain. Place the cream and eggs in a bowl and whisk to
combine. Add the parmesan, mint, mustard, tuna and peas
and mix until combined. Pour into the pastry shell and
bake at 160°C (320°F) for 30 minutes or until set. Cut
into wedges and serve with a green salad. Serves 6.
■ If using frozen peas there is no need to boil them first,
just let them defrost.

tuna and grilled vegetable salad

2 red capsicum (bell pepper), sliced lengthwise
2 zucchini (courgette), sliced lengthwise
1 tablespoon olive oil
1 x 400g (14 oz) can tuna in olive oil, drained
1 red onion, finely sliced
1/2 cup green or black olives
3/4 cup flat-leaf parsley
2 tablespoons olive oil, extra
2 tablespoons white wine vinegar
cracked black pepper and sea salt

Toss the capsicum and zucchini with the olive oil. Cook on
a hot chargrill or barbecue until tender. Combine with the
tuna, onion, olives and parsley. Combine the extra oil,
vinegar, pepper and salt and pour over the salad. Toss to
combine and place on serving plates. Serve with crusty
bread. Serves 4.

balsamic octopus and rocket salad

fish roasted in capers and lemon butter

tomato and garlic stew with prawns

balsamic octopus and rocket salad

1 kg (2 lb) baby octopus ■
1/2 cup (4 fl oz) balsamic vinegar
1/3 cup (2 1/2 fl oz) orange juice
1 tablespoon olive oil
cracked black pepper
1 tablespoon sugar
2 cloves garlic, crushed
200g (7 oz) rocket (arugula)
2 Roma tomatoes, sliced

Remove the heads from the octopus and discard. Cut the tentacles into quarters and rinse. Combine the octopus, balsamic, orange juice, oil, pepper, sugar and garlic in a glass bowl and refrigerate for 3 hours or overnight. Drain the octopus, reserving the marinade. Cook the octopus on a preheated hot chargrill, barbecue or frying pan for 45 seconds on each side or until just cooked and tender. Pour the marinade into a saucepan over high heat and boil until reduced by half.
To serve, place the rocket and tomatoes on plates, top with the octopus and spoon over the juices. Serves 4.
■ You can also use squid (calamari) pieces if baby octopus is not available.

fish roasted in capers and lemon butter

4 x 200g (7 oz) firm white-fleshed fish fillets
2 tablespoons salted capers, rinsed
1 tablespoon finely grated lemon zest
1/2 cup finely grated parmesan cheese
60g (2 oz) butter, softened
cracked black pepper

Preheat the oven to 200°C (400°F). Place the fish fillets in a baking dish lined with non-stick baking paper. Combine the capers, lemon zest, parmesan, butter and pepper. Spread the mixture over the fish. Bake for 20 minutes or until the fish fillets are cooked and the tops are golden. Serve with steamed asparagus and roast potatoes. Serves 4.

tomato and garlic stew with prawns

1 tablespoon olive oil
2 onions, sliced
3 cloves garlic, finely chopped
2 x 440g (14 1/2 oz) cans whole peeled tomatoes
1 cup (8 fl oz) white wine
2 cups (16 fl oz) vegetable or fish stock
500g (1 lb) shelled raw prawns (shrimp) ■
2 tablespoons chopped flat-leaf parsley
cracked black pepper and sea salt

Heat a saucepan over medium heat. Add the oil, onions and garlic and cook, stirring occasionally, for 8 minutes or until soft and golden. Add the tomatoes and crush with a fork. Add the wine and stock and simmer for 10 minutes or until thickened slightly.
Add the prawns and cook for 5 minutes or until they have turned red. Add the parsley, pepper and salt. Spoon into bowls. Serve with crusty bread. Serves 4.
■ You will need 1 kg (2 lb) unshelled prawns to get 500g (1 lb) shelled.

tuna carpaccio with crispy caper dressing

150g (5 oz) rocket (arugula)
200g (7 oz) blanched green beans, whole
300g (10 oz) fresh tuna, thinly sliced
dressing
2 tablespoons olive oil
2 tablespoons salted capers, rinsed
1 tablespoon finely grated lemon zest
2 tablespoons roughly chopped dill sprigs
cracked black pepper

To make the dressing, heat a frying pan over medium to high heat. Add the oil, capers and lemon zest and cook for 4 minutes or until crisp. Remove the pan from the heat and add the dill and pepper. Allow to cool.
Place the rocket, beans and tuna on serving plates, pour over the dressing. Serve with lemon wedges if desired. Serves 4.

tuna carpaccio with crispy caper dressing

short order

balsamic-roasted red onions

basic tomato sauce

garlic roast asparagus

short order

balsamic-roasted red onions

Place 6 halved red onions, cut side up, on a lined baking tray. Loosen the onion layers with your fingers. Sprinkle with balsamic vinegar so that it gets between the onion layers. Sprinkle with sugar and a little olive oil, cover and bake in a preheated oven at 160°C (325°F) for 35 minutes. Remove the cover and bake for a further 25 minutes or until golden. Serve with green leaves and tomatoes as a salad, or use as a pizza topping.

basic tomato sauce

Place a saucepan over medium heat. Add 1 tablespoon olive oil, 2 chopped onions and 2 sliced garlic cloves and cook for 4 minutes. Add 2 x 400g (14 oz) cans whole tomatoes and crush into small pieces with a wooden spoon. Simmer for 5 minutes or until the desired consistency. Add chopped fresh herbs such as parsley, basil or oregano, pepper and sea salt. Serve over pasta, use as a base for pizza, or spoon over cooked meats or fish.

garlic roast asparagus

Place 2–3 bunches trimmed asparagus into a baking dish. Sprinkle over a generous amount of olive oil and then toss with 4 sliced garlic cloves and the shredded zest of 1 lemon. Cover and bake in a preheated oven at 180°C (360°F) for 25–35 minutes or until the asparagus is soft. Serve warm as a side dish or chilled as a salad with a squeeze of lemon and shaved parmesan cheese.

balsamic glaze

Place 2/3 cup (5 fl oz) balsamic vinegar, 1/2 cup brown sugar and 1/2 cup (4 fl oz) water in a saucepan over medium heat. Allow to simmer for 6 minutes or until it thickens slightly. Spoon over grilled steaks, chicken or vegetables or cool and use as a dressing for tomatoes or salad greens.

flavoured olives

Check olives for saltiness and soak in cold water to remove excess salt if necessary. Combine the olives with shredded lemon zest, thyme leaves, cracked black pepper, lemon juice, chopped chillies and olive oil. Allow to marinate for at least 4 hours.

crispy fried capers

These make a great topping for many dishes, including lamb, chicken and fish or even salads. Rinse salted capers under running water and dry well. Place a few tablespoons of olive oil in a frying pan over medium to high heat. Add the capers and cook for 6–8 minutes or until crisp. Drain.

tomato and caper bruschetta

For a simple topping, drain a 400g (14 oz) can of whole tomatoes. Halve the tomatoes and place in a frying pan with 2 tablespoons rinsed salted capers, 1 crushed garlic clove and 2 teaspoons olive oil. Allow to simmer until thick. Top grilled bread with a little olive oil and torn basil leaves. Spoon over the tomato mixture and season with cracked black pepper and sea salt.

flavoured tuna

Combine a 425g (14 oz) can of drained tuna with 1 tablespoon lemon juice, 2 tablespoons olive oil, 2 tablespoons rinsed salted capers, 1 teaspoon finely grated lemon zest, 1/2 finely sliced red onion and 1/2 cup chopped flat-leaf parsley. Spoon onto baguettes or toss through hot or cold pasta.

warm potato and tuna salad

Take 2 large still-warm cooked potatoes and slice thickly. Combine with a 400g (14 oz) can of drained tuna and 150g (5 oz) blanched green beans. To make the dressing, combine 2 tablespoons olive oil with 2 tablespoons white wine vinegar and 1 tablespoon seeded mustard. Pour over the salad and serve.

balsamic glaze

flavoured olives

crispy fried capers

tomato and caper bruschetta

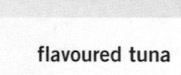

flavoured tuna

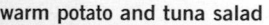

warm potato and tuna salad

107

sweet chilli sauce
hoisin sauce
rice wine

asian

soy sauce
fish sauce
oyster sauce
sesame oil
peanut oil.

basics

sweet chilli and hoisin sauces

These two very versatile sauces offer sweetness with a subtle kick. Sweet chilli sauce is a combination of very mild chopped chillies in a thick sugar syrup and vinegar. It is very much a part of the Asian table and is used as tomato ketchup is in Western societies. Hoisin sauce is a mixture of fermented soybeans, sugar, salt, red rice and spices. It is ideal for stir-fries and marinades.

cooking wine – rice wine

A mild, mellow-tasting wine made from a base of fermented glutinous rice, millet and yeast, rice wine is available in bottles from Asian supermarkets under its Chinese name, 'shao hsing'. It is perfect to use in cooking and complements all meats and strong-flavoured seafood. If you have no cooking wine, you can use medium or dry sherry in its place.

soy, fish and oyster sauces

These salty sauces are essential for Asian cooking. Soy sauce is made from fermented soybeans and the Japanese variety is often more refined than the Chinese. Fish sauce is widely used in Thai and Vietnamese cooking. It has a pungent aroma, and the taste is addictive. The flavour of oyster sauce is indispensable in many Chinese dishes, especially steamed greens and stir-fries. Purchase one that contains premium oyster extract.

oils – sesame and peanut

Sesame oil adds the unique taste of toasted sesame to foods. It has quite a strong flavour, so you only need to add one or two teaspoons at a time. Peanut oil is ideal for deep-frying, shallow-frying or stir-frying over a high temperature – it has a high smoking point, and won't give food the burnt flavour you often get when cooking with other types of oil at high temperature.

tricks + tips

balance

Asian cooking is all about balancing flavours: the sweet, the salty, the hot and the sour. In this style of cooking, the sweetness comes from palm or brown sugar, or sweet chilli sauce; the saltiness from soy, fish and oyster sauces; the heat from chillies and other pungent spices; and the sourness from lemon or lime juice. Aim for a balance of these flavours when cooking Asian-style dishes.

texture

Another important element in Asian cooking is texture. Dishes are often constructed to feature a contrast between different textures (the crispy skin of duck or chicken against its soft braised meat, for example) or to accentuate similar textures (the silkiness of soft tofu in a rich coconut soup). When cooking vegetables, they should retain some of their crunch to add texture to the finished dish.

the sugar to salt ratio

If a dish you are making tastes too salty, use sugar to balance the saltiness. Add the sugar a little at a time, tasting as you go, until a balance is achieved. The reverse also applies: add salt to balance a dish that is too sweet.

stir-fry success

Stir-frying is a frequently used method of cooking in Asian cuisine. The key to successful stir-frying is to have your wok or frying pan smoking hot. To avoid the taste of burnt oil in the food, or too much smoke in the kitchen, heat the dry wok or frying pan over high heat for at least 5 minutes before adding the oil. Allow the oil to heat for 10 seconds before adding the ingredients and stir-frying in small batches to keep the wok or frying pan hot.

beef salad with coconut dressing   seared salmon on coconut spinach

crispy spiced Thai chicken

beef salad with coconut dressing

750g (1 1/2 lb) rump or topside steak, trimmed
2 cups shredded green mango or celery
200g (7 oz) cherry tomatoes, quartered
1 cup coriander (cilantro) leaves
1/2 cup shredded mint leaves
coconut dressing
1/2 cup (4 fl oz) coconut cream
2 tablespoons lime juice
1 tablespoon fish sauce

Heat a frying pan, barbecue or grill (broiler) over high heat. Cook the steak for 2 minutes on each side or until done to your liking. Set aside.
Combine the mango or celery, tomatoes, coriander and mint. Slice the steak thinly and add to the salad, tossing to combine. To make the dressing, combine the coconut cream, lime juice and fish sauce. Divide the dressing between 4 small bowls and serve with the salad. Serves 4.

seared salmon on coconut spinach

4 x 180g (6 oz) salmon fillets
2 teaspoons grated ginger
1 tablespoon sesame oil
2 tablespoons soy sauce
coconut spinach
2 cloves garlic, crushed
2 small red chillies, seeded and chopped
2 tablespoons Asian chilli paste
2 cups (16 fl oz) coconut cream
3 tablespoons lemon juice
2 bunches English spinach, stems removed

Place the salmon in a shallow dish with the ginger, sesame oil and soy. Allow to marinate for 10 minutes on each side. Heat a frying pan over high heat and cook the salmon for 1 minute on each side.
To make the coconut spinach, place the garlic, chillies and chilli paste in a saucepan over medium heat and cook for 2 minutes. Add the coconut cream and lemon juice and simmer for 4 minutes. Add the spinach and toss until wilted.
To serve, place some spinach on each plate and top with a piece of salmon. Serves 4.

crispy spiced Thai chicken

3 chicken breast fillets, quartered
2 egg whites, lightly beaten
3 tablespoons fine rice flour
2 red chillies, seeded and finely chopped
3 tablespoons chopped coriander (cilantro) leaves
4 kaffir lime leaves, shredded
3 tablespoons sesame seeds
2–3 tablespoons peanut oil
watercress sprigs to serve
dipping sauce
3 tablespoons soy sauce
2 tablespoons lemon juice
1 tablespoon brown sugar

Combine the chicken, egg whites, rice flour, chillies, coriander, lime leaves and sesame seeds in a bowl. Heat a frying pan over medium heat. Add the oil and cook the chicken for 3 minutes on each side or until golden and cooked through. Drain on absorbent paper.
To make the dipping sauce, place the soy, lemon juice and sugar in a bowl and mix to combine. Serve the chicken on some watercress with dipping sauce on the side. Serves 4.

Asian-style ribs

1.5 kg (3 lb) or 16 pork spare ribs
marinade
1/2 cup (4 fl oz) hoisin sauce
1 tablespoon grated ginger
1/4 cup (2 fl oz) soy sauce
2 teaspoons sesame oil
1/2 cup (4 fl oz) Chinese rice wine or sherry
1 teaspoon Chinese five-spice powder
2 tablespoons sugar

Preheat the oven to 180°C (350°F). Cut the ribs into individual pieces.
To make the marinade, combine all the ingredients in a large bowl. Add the ribs and toss to coat. Reserve the remaining marinade to brush over the ribs while cooking. Place the ribs on a wire rack in a baking dish. Bake for 20 minutes, then brush with the reserved marinade. Bake for a further 20 minutes or until well browned and crisp. Serve with steamed jasmine rice and greens. Serves 4.

Asian-style ribs

coconut crab soup

chicken and pumpkin stir-fry   twice-cooked crispy chicken

coconut crab soup

200g (7 oz) dried egg noodles
4 cups (2 pints) chicken stock
2 cups (16 fl oz) coconut cream
2 teaspoons grated ginger
4 kaffir lime leaves, shredded
2 small red chillies, seeded and chopped
200g (7 oz) snake or green beans, halved
1 tablespoon peanut oil
2 tablespoons sesame seeds
450g (15 oz) cooked crab meat ▪
1/2 teaspoon cracked black pepper
1/4 cup coriander (cilantro) leaves

Place the noodles in boiling water and set aside for
5 minutes. Drain.
Place the stock, coconut cream, ginger, lime leaves and
chillies in a saucepan over medium heat. Slowly simmer
for 6 minutes. Add the beans and simmer for 7 minutes
or until tender.
While the beans are cooking, heat a frying pan over high
heat and add the oil. Add the sesame seeds and cook for
1 minute. Add the crab, pepper and coriander and cook
for a further 2 minutes or until heated through. To serve,
divide the noodles between 4 bowls, ladle over the soup
and top with the crab mixture. Serves 4.
▪ You can use drained canned crab meat.

chicken and pumpkin stir-fry

2 tablespoons peanut oil
2 onions, sliced
2 small red chillies, seeded and chopped
1/2 teaspoon cracked black pepper
4 chicken breast fillets, sliced
600g (20 oz) pumpkin, peeled and thinly sliced
3 tablespoons fish sauce
1/4 cup small basil leaves

Heat the oil in a preheated frying pan or wok over medium
to high heat. Add the onions, chillies and pepper and cook
for 1 minute. Add the chicken and cook for 3 minutes or
until browned. Add the pumpkin and fish sauce, cover
and cook for 3–4 minutes, stirring occasionally, until the
pumpkin is just soft. Stir through the basil and serve with
steamed jasmine rice. Serves 4.

twice-cooked crispy chicken

1/4 cup (2 fl oz) soy sauce
1/4 cup (2 fl oz) Chinese rice wine
2 tablespoons brown sugar
1 cup (8 fl oz) chicken stock
2 star anise
1 cinnamon stick
4 chicken breast fillets, skin on
2 tablespoons peanut oil

Place the soy, wine, sugar, stock, star anise and cinnamon
stick in a frying pan over medium heat. Allow to simmer
for 4 minutes. Add the breast fillets and cook for
3 minutes on each side. Drain the chicken on a wire
rack and allow to dry.
Heat a clean frying pan over medium to high heat. Add the
oil and chicken, skin side down, and cook for 4 minutes or
until the skin is very crisp. Turn and cook for 1 minute or
until heated through. Slice and serve with steamed greens
and jasmine rice. For added flavour, pour some of the
poaching liquid over the greens. Serves 4.

Thai caramelised pork salad

1/4 cup (2 fl oz) soy sauce
1/2 cup sugar
2 small red chillies, seeded and chopped
1 tablespoon shredded ginger
2 tablespoons fish sauce
2 tablespoons lime juice
1 teaspoon ground star anise
650g (22 oz) boneless pork fillet or tenderloin
salad
100g (3 1/2 oz) salad leaves
4 spring onions (scallions), sliced
1/4 cup basil leaves
1/4 cup mint leaves
1/4 cup coriander (cilantro) leaves

Place the soy, sugar, chillies, ginger, fish sauce, lime
juice and star anise in a deep frying pan over medium
heat and cook, stirring, for 4–5 minutes or until the
mixture thickens slightly. Halve the pork lengthwise and
add to the pan. Cook for 4 minutes on each side or until
tender. Remove the pork from the pan and cool slightly.
Simmer the pan juices until thickened.
To make the salad, toss together the salad leaves, spring
onions, basil, mint and coriander. Slice the pork, drizzle with
the pan juices and serve with the salad. Serves 4.

Thai caramelised pork salad

short order

greens in oyster sauce   dumplings

Thai chicken san choy bau

short order

greens in oyster sauce

Steam halved bok choy, or chopped gai larn (Chinese broccoli), broccoli or green beans over boiling water until tender. Place 2 teaspoons sesame oil in a hot wok with 2 tablespoons shredded ginger and cook for 1 minute. Add 1/3 cup (21/2 fl oz) oyster sauce, 2 tablespoons brown sugar and 1/3 cup (21/2 fl oz) Chinese rice wine and simmer until thick. Place the greens on serving plates and pour over the sauce.

dumplings

Combine 250g (8 oz) minced (ground) chicken or pork with 2 tablespoons sweet chilli sauce, 2 tablespoons hoisin sauce and 2 tablespoons chopped coriander (cilantro). Place small spoonfuls of filling on dumpling wrappers and press the edges to seal. Steam over boiling water or poach in simmering stock for 4 minutes or until cooked. Serve with sweet chilli or hoisin sauce.

Thai chicken san choy bau

Fry 2 chopped red chillies and 500g (1 lb) chicken mince in 1 tablespoon peanut oil in a hot frying pan until golden. Add 2 tablespoons fish sauce, 2 tablespoons lemon juice and 1 tablespoon soy and cook for 1 minute. Remove from the heat and stir through 1/2 cup chopped mixed coriander (cilantro) and mint leaves. Spoon into baby cos lettuce leaves and serve.

Chinese barbecue pork

Replicate the Chinatown favourite. Cut 750g (11/2 lb) pork neck into 5 cm (2 in) wide strips. Combine 1/4 cup (2 fl oz) hoisin sauce, 2 tablespoons soy sauce, 3 tablespoons honey, 11/2 tablespoons Chinese rice wine and 1 teaspoon Chinese five-spice powder. Allow to marinate for at least 3 hours. Place on a rack in a baking dish and bake at 200°C (400°F) for 45 minutes. Slice and use in soups and stir-fries or serve with steamed greens and rice.

Chinatown duck stir-fry

Purchase a barbecued duck from a Chinese barbecue shop. Place 1 tablespoon peanut oil in a hot wok with 2 tablespoons shredded ginger and cook for 1 minute. Chop the duck and add to the wok with 1/2 cup (4 fl oz) Chinese rice wine and 2 tablespoons soy sauce. Serve the duck on steamed greens and spoon over the sauce.

chilli salted snake beans

Place 500g (1 lb) halved snake or green beans in a steamer over boiling water to cook until tender. Place 2 teaspoons sesame oil in a hot wok with 3 chopped large red chillies, 2 sliced garlic cloves, 1/2 teaspoon cracked black pepper and 1/2 teaspoon sea salt. Cook for 2 minutes, then toss with the beans.

tempura prawns

Combine 2 cups fine rice flour with 1 egg and 11/2 cups (12 fl oz) iced water. Stir until smooth. Dip peeled green (raw) prawns (shrimp) into the batter and deep-fry until lightly golden. Drain well and serve with soy or sweet chilli sauce.

spiced tofu

In a frying pan, place 3 tablespoons hoisin sauce, 1/2 cup (4 fl oz) Chinese rice wine, 2 tablespoons shredded ginger, 2 seeded and chopped small red chillies and 1/2 cup (4 fl oz) chicken stock. Simmer for 4 minutes. Add 500g (1 lb) sliced firm tofu and simmer for 3 minutes or until heated through. Serve on steamed greens.

soy and chilli fish

Place 1–2 pieces firm, white-fleshed fish on a heatproof plate that fits inside a bamboo steamer. Sprinkle each piece of fish with 1 tablespoon soy and 1 tablespoon sweet chilli sauce. Place the lid on the steamer and steam over boiling water for 5 minutes or until cooked through. Serve with a green salad or with steamed greens and jasmine rice.

Chinese barbecue pork

Chinatown duck stir-fry

chilli salted snake beans

tempura prawns

spiced tofu

soy and chilli fish

125

asian chilli paste
harissa
green curry paste

pastes

red curry paste
miso paste
dijon mustard
whole grain mustard .

basics

Asian chilli paste and harissa
Asian chilli paste or chilli jam, often labelled 'chilli paste
in soybean oil', is a mixture of ground chillies, shrimp
paste and tamarind. A sweet and mild paste, it can be used
liberally, and is well worth seeking out in Asian supermarkets.
Harissa is a very hot and spicy Middle Eastern chilli paste
that traditionally accompanies couscous. It should be used
sparingly because of its potency.

Thai red and green curry pastes
Despite its colour, red curry paste is milder than the green.
Red curry paste is made from ground red chillies and spices
such as garlic, lemongrass, eschallots, shrimp paste and
ginger. Green curry paste is made from hot green chillies,
coriander (cilantro) and spices. Curry pastes differ in
strength, flavour and heat. I prefer Thai pastes for their
complex flavours, and use them in the recipes in this book.

miso paste

This very thick Japanese paste is made from fermented
soybeans and rice. It has a rich nutty flavour and comes in
a variety of strengths that are distinguished by the miso's
colour: generally, the darker the colour, the stronger the
miso. White miso paste is pale yellow in colour and red
miso paste is dark brown. Miso tends to be a little salty,
so add it to foods gradually and taste as you go.

Dijon and wholegrain mustards

Mustard pastes are made from ground mustard seeds blended
with vinegar and oil. Prepared mustard comes in different
strengths and adds a pungent kick to food. Dijon mustard
is of medium strength, which makes it a good all-round
mustard. If you want an all-round mustard with texture, use
a wholegrain or seeded mustard. Add mustards according
to your taste to dressings, marinades and stuffings.

tricks + tips

maximum flavour

When making a curry, it is best to fry the curry paste first for a few minutes in a hot pan. This toasts the spices in the paste and releases their flavours, giving the finished dish a complex, spicy flavour. Alternatively, add stock or water to the paste and allow to boil for a few minutes or until the spices become fragrant. Do this before adding the other ingredients.

cool it down

If you have added too much curry paste or chilli paste to a dish and it is too hot for your taste, add a little sugar to temper the heat of the chilli. Another way to soften the heat is to serve the dish with a side bowl of thick yoghurt mixed with chopped mint or a cooling salsa of chopped mangoes and mint.

enriching

Use miso paste as you would a stock to enrich the taste of soups, stews and sauces. A teaspoon or two of miso dissolved in hot liquid will make a big difference – it tends to be quite salty, so don't use too much. Add white miso paste where a delicate flavour is required and red miso paste if you need a stronger, richer flavour.

commonscents

The tingling burn you get from mustard is caused by the oils in the mustard seeds. But, unlike chilli, the heat doesn't last long. To check a mustard's strength without having to taste it, just smell it: if the smell tickles your nose, you know you are destined for some heat. Use hot mustards to complement the robust flavours of foods such as roasted meats.

green curry chicken with sweet potato   chilli beef salad

miso-crusted salmon with fennel salad

green curry chicken with sweet potato

1 kg (2 lb) sweet potato, peeled and diced
2 tablespoons peanut oil
2 tablespoons Thai green curry paste
1 tablespoon peanut oil, extra
4 chicken breast fillets
1 cup (8 fl oz) chicken stock
1 cup (8 fl oz) coconut cream
4 kaffir lime leaves, shredded
1/3 cup coriander (cilantro) leaves

Preheat the oven to 200°C (400°F). Place the sweet potato in a baking dish and sprinkle with the oil. Bake for 25 minutes or until golden and soft.
Heat a large frying pan over medium heat. Add the curry paste and extra oil and cook, stirring, for 2 minutes. Add the chicken and cook for 1 minute on each side to seal. Add the stock, coconut cream and lime leaves. Simmer for 15 minutes or until the chicken is tender.
To serve, place the sweet potato on plates and top with the chicken. Spoon over the curry sauce and sprinkle with the coriander leaves. Serve with steamed jasmine rice. Serves 4.

chilli beef salad

1 tablespoon peanut oil
750g (1 1/2 lb) rump or topside steak, trimmed
2–3 tablespoons Asian chilli paste
6 kaffir lime leaves, shredded
1/2 cup chopped roasted unsalted peanuts
salad
1 baby cos lettuce, leaves separated
1/2 cup coriander (cilantro) leaves
1/4 cup small mint leaves
2 tablespoons lime juice
1 tablespoon caster (superfine) sugar

Heat the oil in a frying pan over medium heat. Add the steak and cook for 3–4 minutes on each side or until the beef is well browned and cooked to your liking. Remove and cool. Shred into long, thin strips.
Place a frying pan over medium heat and add the chilli paste and lime leaves and cook for 1 minute. Add the beef strips and toss to coat.
For the salad, combine the lettuce, coriander, mint leaves, lime juice and sugar. Place the salad on plates and top with the beef. Serve sprinkled with the peanuts. Serves 4.

miso-crusted salmon with fennel salad

2 tablespoons white miso paste
1 tablespoon tahini
1 tablespoon sugar
1/3 cup (2 1/2 fl oz) water
4 x 200g (7 oz) pieces fresh salmon or ocean trout
fennel salad
2 small fennel bulbs, very thinly sliced
1 cucumber, shredded
1/4 cup (2 fl oz) lime juice
1 tablespoon fish sauce
2 tablespoons sugar, extra
1/2 cup coriander (cilantro) leaves

Place the miso, tahini, sugar and water in a saucepan and stir over low heat for 2 minutes or until thickened. Heat a non-stick frying pan over medium to high heat. Add the salmon, skin side down, and cook for 3 minutes or until crisp. Brush the salmon with the miso sauce, turn and cook for 1 minute.
For the fennel salad, combine the fennel, cucumber, lime juice, fish sauce, sugar and coriander leaves. To serve, place the fennel salad on plates and top with the salmon. Serve with the remaining miso sauce. Serves 4.

roast lamb with mustard stuffing

2 kg (4 lb) leg of lamb, tunnel-boned ■
6 potatoes, peeled and quartered
olive oil
fresh rosemary
sea salt
stuffing
2 tablespoons Dijon mustard
1 cup fresh breadcrumbs
2 tablespoons honey
2 tablespoons chopped mint

Preheat the oven to 190°C (375°F). Trim the lamb of any excess fat. To make the stuffing, combine the mustard, breadcrumbs, honey and mint. Place the stuffing in the lamb and tie with string to secure.
Place the potatoes in a baking dish, drizzle with olive oil and sprinkle with rosemary and salt. Place a rack over the potatoes and place the lamb on top. Bake for 50–60 minutes or until the lamb and potatoes are tender. Serve with steamed green vegetables. Serves 4.
■ Ask your butcher to tunnel-bone the lamb.

roast lamb with mustard stuffing

miso and soybean soup

harissa and yoghurt baked chicken

miso and soybean soup

1/4 cup (2 oz) white miso paste
1 tablespoon soy sauce
6 cups (2 1/3 pints) water
3 chicken breast fillets, sliced
2 cups frozen soybeans ▪
2 tablespoons toasted sesame seeds

Place the miso, soy and water in a saucepan over medium heat and allow to come to the boil. Add the breast fillets and cook, stirring, for 5 minutes or until the chicken is cooked. Add the soybeans and cook for 3 minutes or until heated through. Spoon into bowls and top with the sesame seeds. Serves 4.
▪ Soybeans are a creamy-tasting green bean available frozen in some supermarkets or at Asian grocers. You can substitute them with broad (fava) beans if preferred.

harissa and yoghurt baked chicken

1.6 kg (3 1/4 lb) chicken, quartered
1 tablespoon cornflour (cornstarch)
1 cup (8 oz) thick plain yoghurt
1 tablespoon harissa or chilli paste
1/3 cup shredded mint
2 teaspoons ground cumin
cracked black pepper and sea salt

Preheat the oven to 200°C (400°F). Make deep slits all over the chicken pieces. Blend together the cornflour, yoghurt, harissa, mint, cumin, pepper and salt. Spread the yoghurt mixture over both sides of the chicken. Place the chicken on a rack in a baking dish. Bake for 25–35 minutes or until the chicken is crisp and golden. Serve warm or cold with a green salad and a squeeze of lemon. Serves 4.

chilli fish with sweet lemon salad

4 x 200g (7 oz) pieces firm white-fleshed fish
2 tablespoons Asian chilli paste
2 tablespoons coriander (cilantro) leaves
1 tablespoon peanut oil
2 cucumbers, sliced, to serve
sweet lemon salad
4 lemons
1/2 cup sugar
1 red chilli, seeded and chopped
1/4 cup chopped mint
cracked black pepper and sea salt

To make the sweet lemon salad, peel the lemons, removing and discarding all the white pith. Chop the flesh into small dice. Combine with the sugar, chilli, mint, pepper and salt. Spread the chilli paste over the fish and sprinkle with the coriander leaves. Heat a non-stick frying pan over medium to high heat. Add the oil and fish and cook for 2–3 minutes on each side or until tender.
To serve, place the cucumber slices on plates and top with the fish. Spoon some lemon salad on the side and serve with a green salad. Serves 4.

duck curry

1.8 kg (3 1/2 lb) duck ■
3 large red chillies, seeded and shredded
1 tablespoon Thai red curry paste
2 1/2 cups (1 pint) chicken stock
1 star anise
1 cinnamon stick
2 cups (16 fl oz) coconut cream

Preheat the oven to 200°C (400°F). Place the duck on a rack in a baking dish and prick the skin all over, especially where it is fatty. Bake for 1 hour or until the duck is a golden brown colour. Set aside to cool.
Place the chillies and curry paste in a frying pan over low heat and cook for 1 minute. Add the stock, star anise and cinnamon and simmer for 3 minutes. Cut the cooked duck into pieces with a sharp pair of scissors and add to the curry with the coconut cream. Simmer for 6 minutes, turning occasionally.
Place some duck and curry sauce in each bowl and serve with steamed jasmine rice. Serves 4.
■ You can use an already barbecued duck from an Asian butcher instead of cooking one yourself.

red curry of swordfish

1 tablespoon Thai red curry paste
1 stalk lemongrass, white part only, finely chopped
1 cup (8 fl oz) water
2 cups (16 fl oz) coconut cream
4 x 200g (7 oz) pieces swordfish or firm white-fleshed fish
1/3 cup whole basil leaves
2 tablespoons lime juice

Place the curry paste, lemongrass and water in a frying pan and simmer over medium to low heat for 5 minutes. Add the coconut cream and simmer for a further 3 minutes. Add the swordfish and cook for 2–3 minutes on each side or until done to your liking. Stir through the basil leaves and lime juice. Serve with steamed jasmine rice and snowpeas (mange tout). Serves 4.

honey and mustard baked pork

4 parsnips, peeled and halved lengthwise
2 tablespoons olive oil
cracked black pepper and sea salt
1/3 cup (2 1/2 fl oz) wholegrain mustard
750g (1 1/2 lb) pork fillet, trimmed
2 tablespoons oregano leaves
1/4 cup (2 fl oz) honey

Preheat the oven to 190°C (375°F). Place the parsnips, cut side up, in a baking dish and sprinkle with the oil, pepper and salt. Bake for 40 minutes or until golden and tender. Spread the mustard on the pork and place on top of the parsnips. Sprinkle with the oregano and drizzle with the honey. Bake for 25–35 minutes or until the pork is tender. Serve with steamed green beans. Serves 4.

chilli fish with sweet lemon salad

red curry of swordfish

duck curry

honey and mustard baked pork

short order

chilli chicken wraps

harissa and lime marinade

sweet potato curry puffs

short order

chilli chicken wraps

Place 1/4 cup (2 fl oz) Asian chilli paste in a frying pan over medium heat. Add 2 cups shredded cooked chicken and cook for 2 minutes or until the chicken is warm and well coated. Place the chicken on flatbread and top with grated carrot and salad. Roll up the bread to enclose the filling and wrap in paper for a portable lunch.

harissa and lime marinade

Place 2 teaspoons harissa, 4 tablespoons lime juice, 4 tablespoons olive oil, 1 teaspoon ground cumin, 1 tablespoon sugar and 2 tablespoons chopped coriander (cilantro) in a bowl and whisk to combine. Use this potent marinade for meats, chicken, fish or vegetables that are destined for the barbecue, grill (broiler) or a hot frying pan.

sweet potato curry puffs

Cook 1 tablespoon peanut oil, 1 chopped onion and 1 tablespoon Thai green curry paste for 1 minute. Add 600g (20 oz) peeled and finely diced sweet potato and 3/4 cup (6 fl oz) coconut cream and cook, covered, for 10 minutes. Add 1/2 cup thawed frozen peas and 2 tablespoons chopped coriander (cilantro) and allow the mixture to cool. Place in the middle of 13 cm (5 in) puff pastry rounds. Press to seal the edges, glaze with beaten egg and bake in an oven preheated to 180°C (350°F) for 20 minutes or until puffed and golden. Serve with yoghurt blended with mint. Makes 12.

pumpkin in miso broth

Place 2 tablespoons white miso paste and 3 cups (24 fl oz) water in a saucepan. Add 750g (1 1/2 lb) peeled and chopped pumpkin. Cover and simmer over low heat until the pumpkin is tender. Serve as a tasty side dish.

miso dressing

Whisk together 2 tablespoons white miso paste with 3 tablespoons olive oil, 1/3 cup (2 1/2 fl oz) water, 1 tablespoon lemon juice and 2 tablespoons tahini. Use as a dressing for salads or steamed vegetables.

honey mustard

Combine 1/2 cup (4 fl oz) Dijon mustard, 1/4 cup (2 oz) brown sugar and 1/4 cup (2 oz) honey in a saucepan and stir over low heat until smooth. Keep cooking and stirring for around 5 minutes or until the sugar and honey have caramelised. Cool then store in the refrigerator. Use on sandwiches and serve with meat and chicken.

hot potato mustard dressing

Combine 2 tablespoons olive oil, 2 tablespoons white wine vinegar and 2 tablespoons wholegrain mustard. Toss with 1 kg (2 lb) warm cooked kipfler potatoes halved lengthwise, 1 finely chopped red onion and 1/4 cup flat-leaf parsley. Serve this warm salad with smoked salmon or prawns.

coconut beef skewers

Slice 750g (1 1/2 lb) trimmed rump or topside steak into long, thick strips and thread onto skewers. Combine 1 tablespoon Thai red curry paste with 1/3 cup (2 1/2 fl oz) coconut cream and 1/4 cup shredded coconut and spread over the meat. Place the skewers on a preheated hot grill (broiler) or barbecue and cook for 2 minutes on each side or until the meat is done to your liking. Serve with a simple salad.

mustard mash

Mash 5 boiled potatoes with butter, sea salt and milk until smooth. Add 1/4 cup (2 fl oz) Dijon mustard and stir through. Serve with grilled steak or roast meats.

pumpkin in miso broth

miso dressing

honey mustard

hot potato mustard dressing

coconut beef skewers

mustard mash

baking powder
bicarbonate of soda
almonds

bake

coconut
plain flour
self-raising flour
cocoa
chocolate
vanilla

basics

baking powder and bicarbonate of soda

When mixed with liquid and heated, baking powder produces small bubbles of carbon dioxide that cause a cake or bread to rise. (It loses its effectiveness after a few months of storage, however.) Bicarbonate of soda (baking soda) is another leavening agent. An alkaline, it reacts with heat and acid to produce carbon dioxide. I prefer to use baking powder – it has a milder taste and leaves no residual flavour in baked goods.

almonds and coconut

These are two of my favourite ingredients. Ground almonds (almond meal) produce a rich, buttery flavour when used in baking. To make almond meal, grind blanched almonds in a food processor. Coconut is readily available desiccated (a fine, dried form) or shredded (also dried, but in larger pieces). Coconut, almonds and other nuts are high in fats and oils, so they make biscuits and cakes moist.

flours – plain and self-raising

Ground white wheat flour, known as plain (all-purpose) flour, is a pantry staple, as is the self-raising (self-rising) variety. You can make your own self-raising flour by adding 1 teaspoon baking powder to 1 cup plain flour. Cornflour (cornstarch) is used to thicken sauces, and also in combination with other flours to give baked goods such as shortbread finer crumb and texture.

cocoa, chocolate and vanilla

When using these three ingredients, remember that the better the quality, the better the flavour. Choose a good-quality non-alkalised cocoa powder with a rich reddish-brown colour. For the best and smoothest chocolate flavour, use a couverture baking chocolate – not a compound one. And for a true vanilla taste, use vanilla extract instead of imitation vanilla essence.

tricks + tips

going nutty

In the summer months, shelled nuts are best kept sealed in the refrigerator so that the oils they contain don't go rancid. In the cooler months you can store them in the pantry. To bring out the flavour of nuts, place them in a single layer on a baking tray and cook in the oven for about 10 minutes at 180°C (350°F) until they turn golden and become fragrant.

sifty business

Before using any kind of flour or cocoa powder when baking, sift it to remove any lumps. In the process of sifting, you also incorporate air with the flour, which makes baked goods lighter and fluffier. Sifted dry ingredients are also less likely to form lumps when combined with liquid.

melting chocolate

Chocolate burns easily, so melt it with care. Use either of the following methods for a smooth result. Chop the chocolate, place in a heatproof bowl and place over a saucepan of boiling water. Stir occasionally until the chocolate is almost smooth. Just before all the chocolate has melted, remove the bowl from the saucepan and continue stirring until smooth. Alternatively, place the bowl in a microwave on medium–low and heat in 1-minute bursts, stirring after each time.

ice perfect

Before icing a cake, chill it – but don't chill the icing or glaze. The icing is easier to control and spread at room temperature, while a chilled cake is easier to smooth the icing onto. It also allows you to make perfect icing 'drips' down the side of a cake. This technique is also valuable on a hot day, as it helps keep fillings such as whipped fresh cream from splitting.

caramel-filled biscuits   simple vanilla cake

frosty lemon cakes

caramel-filled biscuits

250g (8 oz) butter, chopped
1 cup icing (confectioner's) sugar
1½ cups plain (all-purpose) flour, sifted
1 cup cornflour (cornstarch), sifted
1 egg
caramel filling
1 x 400g (14 oz) can sweetened condensed milk
60g (2 oz) butter
2 tablespoons golden syrup

Place the butter, icing sugar, flour, cornflour and egg in
a food processor and process until a smooth dough forms.
Roll tablespoons of the mixture into balls and place on
lined baking trays. Flatten the dough slightly and place
the trays in the refrigerator for 10 minutes or until firm.
Bake the biscuits in a preheated 180°C (350°F) oven for
10–15 minutes or until lightly golden. Cool on racks.
To make the caramel filling, combine the condensed milk,
butter and golden syrup in a heatproof bowl. Place over
a saucepan of boiling water and stir occasionally for
15–20 minutes or until the caramel is thick. Cool the
caramel for 10 minutes, then spoon onto the flat side of
half the biscuits. Top with the remaining biscuits and allow
to cool and become firm. Makes 25.

simple vanilla cake

250g (8 oz) butter
1 cup caster (superfine) sugar
1 teaspoon vanilla extract
3 eggs
2 cups plain (all-purpose) flour, sifted
2½ teaspoons baking powder

Preheat the oven to 160°C (325°F). Line the base of a
20 cm (8 in) square cake tin with non-stick baking paper
and grease the sides. Place the butter and sugar in a
bowl and beat until light and creamy. Add the vanilla
and eggs and beat well. Sift together the flour and baking
powder, and fold into the butter mixture.
Pour the batter into the tin and bake for 1 hour or until
cooked when tested with a skewer. Cool on a wire rack.
To serve, dust with icing (confectioner's) sugar or ice with
whipped vanilla buttercream (page 180). Serves 8–10.

frosty lemon cakes

125g (4 oz) butter, chopped
2 teaspoons grated lemon zest
1 cup caster (superfine) sugar
4 eggs
1¾ cups ground almonds
1 cup self-raising flour, sifted
¼ cup (2 fl oz) lemon juice
¾ cup sugar

Preheat the oven to 160°C (325°F). Place the butter,
lemon zest and sugar in the bowl of an electric mixer
and beat until light and creamy. Gradually add the
eggs and beat well. Lightly fold through the ground
almonds and flour with a wooden spoon. Spoon the
mixture into 12 x ½ cup capacity non-stick muffin
pans and bake for 20 minutes or until the cakes are
golden and cooked when tested with a skewer.
Remove the cakes from the pans while hot. Combine
the lemon juice and sugar, pour a little over each cake,
and allow to stand for 3 minutes before serving warm,
or serve cold. Makes 12.

orange and almond dessert cake

2 oranges, washed
125g (4 oz) butter
1 cup caster (superfine) sugar
5 eggs
2 cups ground almonds
½ cup self-raising flour, sifted
2 teaspoons baking powder
orange syrup
1 cup sugar
2 tablespoons orange juice
1⅓ cups (10½ fl oz) water

Preheat the oven to 180°C (350°F). Line the base of a
22 cm (9 in) tin. Place the oranges in a saucepan of water,
cover and simmer for 10 minutes or until soft. Remove
from the water and chop roughly, removing any seeds.
Process the oranges, butter, sugar, eggs, ground almonds,
flour and baking powder in a food processor until smooth.
Spoon the mixture into the tin and bake for 1 hour or until
cooked when tested with a skewer.
To make the orange syrup, place the sugar, orange juice
and water in a saucepan over medium heat and simmer
for 5 minutes.
To serve, cut the warm cake into wedges and spoon over
some of the syrup. Serve with thick cream. Serves 8–10.

orange and almond dessert cake

raspberry macaroon tarts

easy chocolate cake

peach and raspberry tart

baked winter fruits

raspberry macaroon tarts

3 egg whites
3/4 cup sugar
3 cups desiccated coconut
filling
1/2 cup (4 fl oz) cream
125g (4 oz) dark chocolate, chopped
2 eggs
2 tablespoons caster (superfine) sugar
2 tablespoons self-raising flour, sifted
200g (7 oz) raspberries ▪

Preheat the oven to 140°C (280°F). Combine the egg whites, sugar and coconut to make the macaroon mixture and divide between 6 x 8 cm (3¼ in) well-oiled tart tins with removable bases. Press firmly over the base and sides. Bake for 25–30 minutes or until the macaroon is firm.
To make the filling, place the cream and chocolate in a saucepan over low heat and stir until smooth. Set aside. Place the eggs and sugar in the bowl of an electric mixer and beat until light and creamy. Fold through the flour and chocolate mixture. Spoon the mixture into the macaroon shells and top with the raspberries. Bake at 160°C (325°F) for 25 minutes or until the filling is just firm. Cool in the tins. Serves 6.
▪ You can use unthawed frozen raspberries to top the tarts if you prefer.

peach and raspberry tart

125g (4 oz) butter, softened
1 cup caster (superfine) sugar
1 teaspoon vanilla extract
2 eggs
1½ cups self-raising flour, sifted
2 peaches, halved and cut into thin wedges
150g (5 oz) raspberries ▪
2 tablespoons icing (confectioner's) sugar

Preheat the oven to 160°C (325°F). Line a 22 cm (9 in) round cake tin with a removable base with baking paper. Place the butter, sugar and vanilla in the bowl of an electric mixer and beat until light and creamy. Add the eggs and beat well. Fold in the flour and spoon the mixture into the tin. Top with the peaches and raspberries and sprinkle with the icing sugar.
Bake for 1 hour or until the tart is cooked when tested with a skewer. Remove from the tin and serve warm in wedges with vanilla bean ice-cream. Serves 8–10.
▪ You can use unthawed frozen raspberries to top the tart if you prefer.

easy chocolate cake

250g (8 oz) butter
1⅓ cups brown sugar
3 eggs
2 cups plain (all-purpose) flour, sifted
1½ teaspoons baking powder
1/3 cup cocoa powder, sifted
1 cup (8 fl oz) sour cream
250g (8 oz) dark chocolate, melted
chocolate glaze
150g (5 oz) dark chocolate, chopped
1/3 cup (2½ fl oz) cream

Preheat the oven to 160°C (325°F). Grease a 22 cm (9 in) round cake tin. Place the butter and sugar in the bowl of an electric mixer and beat until light and creamy. Add the eggs and beat well. Sift the flour, baking powder and cocoa over the butter mixture, add the sour cream and chocolate, and mix until just combined.
Pour the mixture into the tin and bake for 55 minutes to 1 hour or until just set. Cool in the tin.
To make the chocolate glaze, combine the chocolate and cream in a saucepan over low heat and stir until smooth. Allow the glaze to stand for 5 minutes before spreading over the top of the cake. Serves 8–10.

baked winter fruits

300g (10 oz) blackberries
500g (1 lb) chopped rhubarb
3 red apples, cored and sliced
1/2 cup caster (superfine) sugar
marsala custard
1 cup (8 fl oz) marsala*
2 cups (16 fl oz) cream
4 egg yolks
1/4 cup sugar

Preheat the oven to 180°C (350°F). Combine the blackberries, rhubarb, apples and sugar and place in 6 x 1 cup capacity ovenproof dishes. Bake for 25–30 minutes or until the fruit is soft.
To make the custard, place the marsala and cream in a saucepan over medium heat. Heat the mixture until it is hot but not boiling. Continue to heat for 5 minutes or until reduced slightly. Remove from the heat and whisk in the egg yolks and sugar. Return the mixture to the heat and stir over low heat for 10 minutes, until the custard thickens. Serve the custard and baked fruits warm. Serves 6.

brown sugar almond biscotti

2 cups plain (all-purpose) flour, sifted
1 1/2 teaspoons baking powder
3/4 cup dark brown sugar
3/4 cup blanched whole almonds
2 eggs, lightly beaten
1 teaspoon vanilla extract

Preheat the oven to 160°C (325°F). Place the flour, baking powder, sugar and almonds in a bowl and mix to combine. Add the eggs and vanilla and mix well until a soft dough forms – this will take a while, as the dough needs to be worked so that it stays together. Place the dough on a lightly floured surface and knead until smooth. Divide the dough into 2 logs and flatten slightly. Place the logs on a greased baking tray and bake for 30 minutes. Remove from the oven and allow to cool completely.
Slice the logs into 5 mm (1/4 in) thick slices and place on a lined baking tray. Bake for 10–15 minutes or until the biscotti are crisp. Store in an airtight container and serve with espresso coffee for dunking or with ice-cream or a dessert. Makes 45.

baked ricotta cakes

1/2 cup (4 fl oz) marsala*
1/3 cup sultanas
750g (1 1/2 lb) fresh ricotta
6 eggs
3 tablespoons cornflour (cornstarch), sifted
1 1/4 cups caster (superfine) sugar

Preheat the oven to 160°C (325°F). Place the marsala and sultanas in a saucepan over low heat and simmer for 5 minutes. Set aside to cool.
Place the ricotta, eggs, cornflour and sugar in a food processor and process until smooth. Stir in the sultana mixture. Pour the mixture into 12 x 1/2 cup capacity greased non-stick muffin tins, filling them to the top. Bake for 30–35 minutes or until firm. Cool in the tins. Serves 12.

pear pancakes

2 cups self-raising flour, sifted
1 teaspoon baking powder
1/4 cup caster (superfine) sugar
3 eggs, lightly beaten
3 cups (24 fl oz) buttermilk
60g (2 oz) butter, melted
sweet pears
2 firm pears, peeled
45g (1 1/2 oz) butter, melted
caster (superfine) sugar, extra

Place the flour, baking powder and sugar in a bowl. Combine the eggs, buttermilk and butter and whisk into the flour mixture until smooth.
To make the sweet pears, cut into 1.5 cm (2/3 in) slices. Brush both sides of the pears with the melted butter and sprinkle with the sugar. Place a slice of pear in a non-stick frying pan over medium heat. Cook for 1 minute on each side or until golden. Spoon 1/3–1/2 cup pancake mixture over the pear and cook for 2–3 minutes on each side or until the pancake is golden and fluffy. Serve the pancakes with maple syrup and butter. Serves 6.

cinnamon pear pies

4 firm pears, peeled and left whole
1 cup sugar
2 cinnamon sticks
4 cups (2 pints) water
filling
3/4 cup caster (superfine) sugar
40g (1 1/2 oz) butter, softened
1/2 teaspoon vanilla extract
3/4 cup (6 fl oz) cream
2 eggs, separated
1 cup ground almonds
1/4 cup self-raising flour, sifted

Place the pears, sugar, cinnamon and water in a saucepan. Cover and simmer over low heat for 15–20 minutes or until the pears are just soft. Allow to cool.
Preheat the oven to 180°C (350°F). To make the filling, place the sugar, butter, vanilla, cream, egg yolks, ground almonds and flour in the bowl of an electric mixer and beat until thick and smooth. Beat the egg whites in a clean bowl until soft peaks form. Fold the egg whites into the mixture and spoon into the base of 4 x 1 1/2 cup capacity ovenproof dishes. Top with a pear and press so that one-third of the pear is submerged in the mixture. Bake for 25–30 minutes or until the filling is firm. Serve warm with ice-cream on the side. Serves 4–6.

brown sugar almond biscotti

pear pancakes

baked ricotta cakes

cinnamon pear pies

157

short order

no-fuss blueberry muffins

raspberry upside-down cakes

simple shortbread

short order

no-fuss blueberry muffins

In a bowl, combine 2 cups sifted self-raising flour, 1/2 cup caster (superfine) sugar, 2 eggs, 1/3 cup (2 1/2 fl oz) vegetable oil and 1 cup (8 fl oz) sour cream and mix well. Sprinkle the mixture with 1 cup fresh or unthawed frozen blueberries and then spoon into 1 cup capacity muffin tins. Bake in a preheated 180°C (350°F) oven for 25–30 minutes or until cooked through.

raspberry upside-down cakes

Prepare a quantity of the simple vanilla cake on page 152. Grease 18 x 1/2 cup capacity muffin tins and divide 300g (10 oz) fresh or unthawed frozen raspberries among the bases. Spoon over the batter and bake in a preheated 160°C (325°F) oven for 20 minutes or until puffed and golden. Cool in the tins for 5 minutes, then invert onto a wire rack.

simple shortbread

Place 180g (6 oz) chopped butter, 3/4 cup caster (superfine) sugar, 1 cup sifted cornflour (cornstarch), 1 1/2 cups sifted plain (all-purpose) flour and 1 egg in a food processor and process until a smooth dough forms. Press the mixture into a lined shallow 20 cm x 30 cm (8 in x 12 in) tin. Score the top of the shortbread into long bars. Bake in a preheated 160°C (325°F) oven for 35–40 minutes or until golden. Cool in the tin.

food-processor cookies

Process 125g (4 oz) softened butter, 1/2 teaspoon vanilla extract, 1 cup brown sugar, 1 egg, 1/4 cup (2 fl oz) milk, 2 cups plain (all-purpose) flour and 1 teaspoon baking powder in a food processor until smooth. Place in a bowl and stir through 1/2 cup rolled oats, 3/4 cup raisins and 1 cup chocolate chips. Place in 2-tablespoon heaps on a lined and greased baking tray and bake in a preheated 180°C (350°F) oven for 12–15 minutes or until golden. Makes 25.

pear and almond galettes

Cut ready-rolled puff pastry into 15 cm (6 in) squares. Sprinkle ground almonds over and top with thin slices of pear, leaving a border around the edge. Brush the pear with melted butter and sprinkle with demerara sugar. Bake in a preheated 180°C (350°F) oven for 20 minutes or until golden.

food-processor banana cake

Place 1 cup caster (superfine) sugar, 1/4 cup brown sugar, 1 cup mashed banana, 125g (4 oz) melted butter, 3 eggs and 3/4 cup (6 fl oz) sour cream in a food processor and process until smooth. Add 1 3/4 cups self-raising flour and process until combined. Spoon the mixture into a 25 cm (10 in) fluted ring tin and bake in a preheated 180°C (350°F) oven for 40 minutes or until cooked.

vanilla and coconut baked apples

Core large apples, scooping out some of the flesh, and score around the middle of the skin. Make a filling of 1/2 cup desiccated coconut, 1 tablespoon plain (all-purpose) flour, 60g (2 oz) soft butter and 3 tablespoons demerara sugar. Spoon into the apples and top with a piece of vanilla bean. Bake in a preheated 180°C (350°F) oven for 40 minutes or until soft.

basic and speedy brownie

Melt 250g (8 oz) butter and process with 1 1/3 cups sifted plain (all-purpose) flour, 2 1/4 cups sugar, 3/4 cup sifted cocoa powder, 4 eggs and 1/4 teaspoon baking powder in a food processor until smooth. Pour into a lined 20 cm (8 in) square cake tin and bake at 170°C (330°F) for 50 minutes.

simple crumble

Top sliced fruit with a mixture of 3/4 cup brown sugar, 1 cup rolled oats, 1/2 cup plain (all-purpose) flour and 100g (3 1/2 oz) soft butter. Bake in a preheated 180°C (350°F) oven for 35 minutes or until golden brown.

food-processor cookies

pear and almond galettes

food-processor banana cake

vanilla and coconut baked apples

simple crumble

basic and speedy brownie

honey
white sugar
caster sugar
icing sugar

sweet

maple syrup
brown sugar
dark brown sugar
demerara sugar

basics

honey

A sweet and thick liquid that is made by bees from flower nectar and stored in their hives in a maze of waxy honeycomb. In general, the darker the honey, the stronger the flavour. Most commercially produced honey has been pasteurised and purified. Any mild-flavoured honey is suitable for baking or flavouring foods, and adds a sweet dimension different from sugar.

white, caster and icing sugar

These are all white sugars of differing texture. Normal or granulated sugar has the largest grains. Caster (superfine) sugar granules are about half the size of normal sugar and are used in baking because they dissolve easily when heated. Icing (confectioner's) sugar is sugar that has been crushed to a fine powder. It dissolves easily in a little water to make a smooth paste that can be used as icing.

maple syrup

The caramelised sap of maple trees (which are native to North America and tapped for their sap at the end of winter). It is available as a thin amber liquid and is traditionally used on pancakes, but also bakes well. Imitation maple syrup is available at a cheaper price, but the taste is inferior to the real thing.

brown, dark brown and demerara sugar

As their colour suggests, these sugars have residual molasses that has not been removed during processing, and which gives them their caramel taste. Both brown and dark brown sugars are soft and moist, have a small grain and are easily dissolved when mixed with liquid or heated. Demerara sugar has harder and drier crystals, and a mild caramel taste. All are suitable for use in baking.

tricks + tips

spoon brûlée

To successfully brûlée the top of a tart or custard, you will need a brûlée iron (available from cooking supply stores). Alternatively, you can heat a large metal kitchen spoon over a gas cooktop flame until it is red-hot. Wearing an oven mitt, remove the hot spoon from the cooktop and run it over the sugar on top of the tart in a circular motion until it becomes golden and caramelised.

sugar syrup

To make a simple sugar syrup, place some sugar and water in a saucepan and stir over low heat, without boiling, until the sugar dissolves. Increase the heat to a slow boil and, at this point, brush the sides of the saucepan with a wet pastry brush to remove any sugar crystals caught on the side. Simmer the syrup until it is of the desired consistency or until a golden caramel forms.

pure sweetness

The pure form of icing sugar (confectioner's sugar) often needs to be sifted before use, unlike icing sugar mixture, which contains a starch to stop it from clumping. Although it doesn't need as much sifting, icing sugar mixture doesn't have as pure a taste as icing sugar. Always use pure icing sugar for icing cakes; pure or icing sugar mixture may be used in baking.

runny honey

When measuring honey, first grease the jug you are using with a little oil. This ensures that all the honey will run from the jug easily. If honey crystallises or turns thick while being stored, bring it back to a pouring consistency by heating in a microwave oven for a few seconds or by heating the jar in a bowl of hot water.

burnt vanilla creams

toffee apples

honey cakes

burnt vanilla creams

2 cups (16 fl oz) cream
1½ tablespoons cornflour (cornstarch)
5 egg yolks
1 teaspoon vanilla extract
⅓ cup brown sugar
caster (superfine) sugar to top

Place the cream in a saucepan over low heat and allow to become hot but not boil. Whisk together the cornflour, egg yolks, vanilla and brown sugar until smooth. Whisk the egg yolk mixture into the hot cream. Stir over low heat until the mixture thickens. Pour into 1 cup capacity dishes and chill for 3 hours or until firm.
Top with a little caster sugar and either grill (broil) under a very hot grill (broiler) or brûlée with a hot spoon (see page 166). Serves 4.

toffee apples

4 small apples, peeled
4 cups (2 pints) water
1 cup sugar
toffee
1½ cups sugar
½ cup (4 fl oz) water

Place the apples, water and sugar in a saucepan over medium heat and allow to simmer for 4 minutes or until the apples just begin to soften – they should still have crunch to them. Place the apples on a wire rack to cool and dry.
To make the toffee, place the sugar and water in a saucepan and stir over low heat until the sugar has dissolved. Allow to simmer until the toffee is a light golden colour.
Dip the apples in the toffee and place on non-stick baking paper for 5 minutes to set. Serve with thick cream. Serves 4.
■ For hints on making toffee see page 180.

honey cakes

185g (6 oz) butter, softened
⅔ cup caster (superfine) sugar
3 tablespoons honey
2 eggs
1½ cups plain (all-purpose) flour, sifted
1 teaspoon baking powder
icing
1 cup (8 fl oz) thick (double) cream
chilled honey

Preheat the oven to 160°C (325°F). Place the butter, sugar and honey in a bowl and beat until light and creamy. Add the eggs, one at a time, and beat well. Fold the flour and baking powder into the butter mixture.
Spoon the mixture into 12 x ½ cup capacity lightly greased non-stick muffin tins. Bake in the oven for 15–20 minutes or until cooked when tested with a skewer. Cool the cakes on wire racks. Spread the cakes with the cream. Before serving, drizzle with the chilled honey. Makes 12 small cakes.

quince tart tatin

3 quinces, peeled and cored ■
2 cups (16 fl oz) water
1 cup sugar
4 pieces lemon zest
80g (2½ oz) butter, divided into 4 lots
350g (12 oz) ready-rolled puff pastry

Slice the quinces into 2–3 cm (1 in) slices. Heat a large frying pan over medium to high heat. Add the quinces, water, sugar and lemon zest, and cover and cook for 45 minutes or until the quinces are ruby-coloured and soft. Simmer the quinces, uncovered, for 10 minutes to reduce the syrup and to caramelise the juices. Remove the lemon zest and divide the quinces and their pan juices between 4 x 14 cm (5½ in) frying pans. Top each with a piece of butter. Or you can use 1 x 25 cm (10 in) pan. Preheat the oven to 200°C (400°F). Roll out the pastry on a lightly floured surface. Divide into 4 and place over the quinces to cover the top of the pans. Tuck in the pastry edges to neaten. Bake for 15–20 minutes or until the pastry is golden. (If using a large pan, bake for 35 minutes.)
To serve, turn out onto plates and serve with vanilla bean ice-cream. Serves 4.
■ You can also use apples or pears – just reduce the simmering time.

quince tart tatin

milk puddings with rosewater syrup

1½ tablespoons powdered gelatine
3 tablespoons water
3 cups (24 fl oz) milk
1 vanilla bean, split and scraped
⅓ cup caster (superfine) sugar
rosewater syrup
¾ cup (6 fl oz) water
½ cup sugar
1 teaspoon rosewater*

Place the gelatine and water in a saucepan over low heat and stir until the gelatine has dissolved. Add the milk, vanilla bean and sugar and heat for 5 minutes. Remove the vanilla bean and pour the mixture into 6 x ½ cup capacity ramekins or moulds and refrigerate for 4 hours or overnight. To make the rosewater syrup, place the water and sugar in a saucepan and stir over medium heat until the sugar has dissolved. Simmer for 3 minutes. Add the rosewater and cool.
To serve, unmould the puddings onto plates and spoon over the rosewater syrup. Serves 6.

maple cream tart

375g (12½ oz) ready-rolled sweet shortcrust pastry*
2 tablespoons caster (superfine) sugar
filling
1 tablespoon cornflour (cornstarch)
1¾ cups (14 fl oz) cream
½ cup (4 fl oz) maple syrup
5 egg yolks

Roll out the pastry on a lightly floured surface or on a sheet of non-stick baking paper until 3 mm (⅛ in) thick. Line a 22 cm (9 in) pastry ring with the pastry, easing it into the shell without stretching it. Chill for 5 minutes. Blind bake the pastry: prick the base and the sides with a fork and line with a sheet of non-stick baking paper; fill the tin with baking weights or dried beans or rice. Bake the pastry case in a preheated 190°C (375°F) oven for 5 minutes. Remove the weights, beans or rice and paper, and return the pastry to the oven for a further 5 minutes or until it is light golden in colour.
To make the filling, place the cornflour in a bowl and whisk with a little of the cream until the mixture is smooth. Add the remaining cream, maple syrup and egg yolks and whisk until combined.
Pour the filling into the pastry case and bake in a preheated 160°C (325°F) oven for 30–35 minutes or until the filling is set. Chill until cold and set. Sprinkle the top with the sugar and caramelise the top with a brûlée iron or hot metal spoon (see page 166) or under a very hot grill (broiler). Serve in wedges. Serves 8.

choc honey snaps

125g (4 oz) butter
1 cup (8 fl oz) honey
1 teaspoon bicarbonate of soda (baking soda)
2 cups plain (all-purpose) flour
¾ cup caster (superfine) sugar
choc topping
⅓ cup (2½ fl oz) cream
250g (8 oz) milk chocolate, chopped

Preheat the oven to 180°C (350°F). Place the butter and honey in a saucepan over low heat and stir to melt. Add the bicarbonate of soda and remove from the heat. Place the flour and sugar in a bowl, add the butter mixture and mix to combine. Place tablespoons of the mixture onto lined baking trays. Bake for 10–12 minutes or until golden. Cool on trays.
To make the choc topping, place the cream and chocolate in a saucepan over low heat and stir until smooth. Cool slightly before spooning a heaped teaspoon onto each honey snap. Allow to set. Makes 35.

honey and nougat semi freezo

2 cups (16 fl oz) cream
2 eggs, separated
¼ cup (2 fl oz) honey
⅔ cup icing (confectioner's) sugar
150g (5 oz) soft nougat, chopped
¼ cup blanched almonds, roasted and chopped

Place the cream in a bowl and whisk until soft peaks form. Set aside. Place the egg yolks, honey and ¼ cup of the icing sugar in the bowl of an electric mixer and beat until pale and thick. Set aside.
Place the egg whites in the bowl of an electric mixer and beat until soft peaks form. Gradually add the remaining icing sugar and beat until glossy.
Add the egg yolk mixture, egg whites, nougat and almonds to the cream and carefully fold to combine. Place 12 egg rings on a baking tray lined with non-stick paper. Spoon the mixture into the egg rings and freeze for 2 hours or until just solid. (If the semi freezo becomes too hard, transfer to the refrigerator to soften slightly for 30 minutes before serving.) Run a knife around the edges to remove and serve on chilled plates. Serves 4.

milk puddings with rosewater syrup

choc honey snaps

maple cream tart

honey and nougat semi freezo

brown sugar meringues with sugared figs

caramel fig loaf

maple cake

brown sugar meringues with sugared figs

4 egg whites
3/4 cup caster (superfine) sugar
1/2 cup brown sugar
1 tablespoon cornflour (cornstarch)
1 teaspoon white vinegar
8 figs, halved
extra caster (superfine) sugar
thick (double) cream to serve

Preheat the oven to 120°C (250°F). Line a baking tray with non-stick baking paper.
Place the egg whites in the bowl of an electric mixer and beat until soft peaks form. Gradually beat in the sugars, a little at a time. Sift cornflour over the mixture and fold through with the vinegar.
Take 1/2 cup of the mixture and shape into a small round on the baking tray. Repeat with the remaining mixture. Place the tray in the oven and cook for 30–35 minutes. Turn off the oven and allow the meringues to cool in the oven. Press the cut side of the figs into the extra caster sugar. Heat a non-stick frying pan over high heat and add the figs, cut side down, and cook for 2 minutes or until the sugar has melted and is golden. Place the meringues on plates and serve with a spoonful of cream and the figs on the side. Serves 8.

caramel fig loaf

125g (4 oz) butter
1/2 cup demerara sugar
2 eggs
1 1/2 cups plain (all-purpose) flour, sifted
1 teaspoon baking powder
1 teaspoon ground cinnamon
1/4 cup (2 fl oz) golden syrup
250g (8 oz) soft dried figs, sliced

Preheat the oven to 160°C (325°F). Grease and line a 20 cm x 10 cm (8 in x 4 in) loaf tin.
Place the butter and sugar in the bowl of an electric mixer and beat until light and creamy. Add the eggs and beat well. With a wooden spoon, stir through the flour, baking powder, cinnamon, golden syrup and figs. Pour into the tin and bake for 1 hour. Cool on a wire rack.
Serve in slices for afternoon tea or toast thick slices for breakfast or brunch. Serves 6.

maple cake

250g (8 oz) butter, softened
3/4 cup brown sugar
1/2 cup (4 fl oz) maple syrup
4 eggs
2 cups self-raising flour
maple cream
300 ml (10 fl oz) thick (double) cream
2 tablespoons maple syrup

Preheat the oven to 180°C (350°F). Line and grease a 20 cm (8 in) round cake tin.
Place the butter, brown sugar, maple syrup, eggs and flour in the bowl of an electric mixer and beat until combined. Continue to beat for 4 minutes longer or until the mixture turns pale. Pour the mixture into the tin and bake for 50–55 minutes or until cooked when tested with a skewer. Stand in the tin for 10 minutes, then cool on a wire rack.
To make the maple cream, combine the cream and maple syrup and gently whisk until just thick.
Cut the cake in half lengthwise. Spread the cream between the cake layers and over the top. Serves 8–10.

steamed golden syrup puddings

6 tablespoons golden syrup
2 cups self-raising flour
175g (6 oz) butter, softened
3 eggs
1/2 teaspoon vanilla extract
1 cup brown sugar
2 tablespoons golden syrup, extra
thick (double) cream to serve

Place 1 tablespoon of golden syrup in the base of 6 x 1 cup capacity greased pudding dishes. Place the flour, butter, eggs, vanilla, sugar and extra golden syrup in the bowl of an electric mixer and beat until well combined. Spoon the mixture into the pudding dishes and place a round of greaseproof paper over the top of each. Place tight-fitting lids on top of the dishes, or secure a round of greaseproof paper or aluminium foil over them. Place in 2 saucepans and add enough boiling water to come halfway up their sides. Cover and boil for 1 hour or until the puddings are springy to the touch.
Unmould the dishes onto serving plates and serve with cream. Serves 6.

steamed golden syrup puddings

short order

half-sugar jam

flavoured sugar

whipped chocolate buttercream

short order

half-sugar jam

Chop ripe fruit and weigh. Add half the fruit's weight in sugar and place in a large bowl with flavourings such as vanilla beans or cinnamon sticks. Microwave on high in 10-minute bursts until the jam is thick. Because the jam only has half the sugar, it needs to be stored in the refrigerator. This jam can also be made on the stovetop.

flavoured sugar

To flavour sugar, place 1 cup sugar and either 2 cinnamon sticks, 2 vanilla beans or 1 tablespoon freshly grated nutmeg in a food processor and process until finely ground. Stir the mixture through a fine sieve to remove any large pieces. Use cinnamon sugar on pancakes or French toast, vanilla sugar on fresh fruit, and nutmeg sugar in eggnog or on hot buttered toast.

whipped chocolate buttercream

Make the whipped vanilla buttercream (right), then fold through 200g (7 oz) melted and cooled dark chocolate. Do not refrigerate the icing before spreading over the cake.

caramel yoghurt

A very simple but tasty accompaniment to fruit and pancakes. To make, sprinkle brown sugar over thick plain yoghurt and wait a few seconds for it to melt into a caramel syrup.

caramel icing

Place 1/2 cup brown or dark brown sugar in a saucepan with 1 cup (8 fl oz) cream, 1 tablespoon butter and 1 tablespoon water. Stir over medium to low heat until the sugar dissolves, then allow the mixture to simmer for 7 minutes or until thick. Cool until the icing is thick, then spoon over a cake.

baked toffee

Line a 24 cm x 34 cm (9½ in x 13 in) baking tray with non-stick paper. Sprinkle the paper thinly with 1/2 cup caster (superfine) sugar. Place in a 200°C (425°F) oven and bake for 10–12 minutes or until golden. Allow to cool in the tray, then break into pieces. Use to top smooth custard-based dishes or serve with ice-cream.

coloured sugar

Place 1 cup caster (superfine) sugar in a sieve and add a few drops of food colouring. Stir the sugar through the sieve twice or until the colour is evenly distributed. Use to sprinkle on top of iced cup cakes and cookies for instant sparkle.

whipped vanilla buttercream

Place 1 cup icing (confectioner's) sugar and 4 egg whites in the bowl of an electric mixer and beat until soft peaks form. Add 400g (14 oz) chilled, diced butter, a little at a time. The mix may look curdled, but keep beating. Stir through 1 teaspoon vanilla extract. Allow to stand somewhere cool if not using immediately. Do not refrigerate the icing before spreading over the cake.

raspberry sorbet

Make a sugar syrup by placing 2 cups (16 fl oz) water, 1/4 cup (2 fl oz) glucose and 3/4 cup caster (superfine) sugar in a saucepan over medium heat and stir to dissolve. Once dissolved, simmer for 1 minute then refrigerate to cool. To make a sorbet, combine the syrup and 2 cups (16 fl oz) finely strained raspberry purée and 1 tablespoon lemon juice. Pour into an ice-cream machine and churn according to the manufacturer's instructions until the sorbet is firm and scoopable.

caramel yoghurt

caramel icing

baked toffee

coloured sugar

whipped vanilla buttercream

raspberry sorbet

181

glossary

arborio rice
See page 34.

balsamic vinegar
See page 89.

bamboo steamer
A woven bamboo container with a lid and slatted base, used for steaming Asian-style dishes. Meats, vegetables or noodles are placed inside and the steamer is set over a saucepan of boiling water. Available from Asian food stores and cookery shops.

beef stock
See stock.

blanching
A cooking method used to slightly soften the texture, heighten the colour and enhance the flavour of food. It involves plunging food such as vegetables into boiling unsalted water for a few seconds or minutes, then removing it and refreshing it under cold water.

bocconcini
Fresh Italian mozzarella balls, available in a variety of sizes, usually made from cows' milk. Sold in water or a brine solution in delicatessens and supermarkets.

bok choy
This mildly flavoured green is also known as Chinese chard or Chinese white cabbage. Cook baby bok choy whole after washing it well. If using the larger type of bok choy, separate the leaves and trim the dark green ones to leave only the narrow border along the white leaf rib. Limit the cooking to a maximum of a few minutes so that the vegetable stays green and slightly crisp.

capers
See page 88.

carnaroli
See page 34.

chicken stock
See stock.

chilli paste
See page 128.

chinese barbecued duck
Spiced and barbecued duck prepared in the traditional Chinese style is available from Chinese barbecue shops or Chinese food stores.

chinese barbecued pork
Spiced and barbecued pork prepared in the traditional Chinese style is available from Chinese barbecue shops or from Chinese food stores. See page 124 to make your own.

chinese broccoli
Also known as gai larn or Chinese kale, Chinese broccoli is a leafy vegetable with dark green leaves, small white flowers and stout stems (the part of the plant that is most often eaten). Wash thoroughly, peel and split the tough stems, then steam, braise, boil or stir-fry.

chinese cooking wine
See page 110.

chinese five-spice powder
This mellow combination of cinnamon, anise pepper, star anise, clove and fennel is great with meats, chicken or seafood. Available from most supermarkets.

chocolate, melting
See page 148.

couscous
See page 71.

cream
Pouring cream (also called single or medium cream) is referred to in this book as 'cream'; it has a butterfat content of 20–30 per cent. Thick or double cream, which is thick enough to be spoonable, has a butterfat content of 45–55 per cent.

demerara sugar
See page 165.

du puy lentils
See page 71.

fish sauce
See page 111.

fish stock
See stock.

gai larn
See Chinese broccoli.

harissa
See page 128.

hoisin sauce
See page 110.

jap pumpkin
This pumpkin is popular because of its thin skin, soft flesh and a sweetness that intensifies with cooking. It has a distinctive green-and-white striped skin and moist, bright-orange flesh.

kaffir lime leaves
Fragrant leaves used crushed or shredded in Thai dishes. Available fresh (which I prefer) or dried in packets from Asian food stores and some greengrocers.

kecap manis
A very thick and sweet but salty Indonesian soy sauce used as a condiment or dipping sauce. Available from Asian food stores.

lemongrass
A tall, lemon-scented grass used in Asian cooking, and particularly Thai dishes. Peel away the outer leaves and chop the tender root-end finely, or add in large pieces during cooking and remove before serving. Available from Asian food stores and some greengrocers.

liquid glucose
A thick viscous syrup made from pure glucose or dextrose. Can be substituted with light corn syrup.

marsala
A dark, sweet, aged Italian sherry used in cooking. It is rich and complex in flavour and can be substituted with any good-quality dark sweet sherry.

melting chocolate
See page 148.

miso paste
See page 129.

noodles
Bean thread, Chinese wheat, egg, ramen, rice and somen. See pages 52–53.

nori sheets
Dried seaweed pressed into square sheets. Used in Japanese-style dishes. Available in packets from Asian food stores.

ovenproof dishes
See tins, moulds and baking dishes.

palm sugar
Palm tree sap concentrated into a heavy, moist sugar. Commonly used in Thai cooking, palm sugar is sold in blocks. Grate or shave portions off to use in cooking. If you want a stronger caramel flavour, buy the darker type, and substitute brown sugar if palm sugar is not available.

pancetta
A cured and rolled Italian-style meat that is like prosciutto but less salty and with a softer texture. It adds a rich flavour when cooked and can be eaten uncooked in thin slices.

pasta
Angel hair, fettuccine, linguine, maccheroni, orecchiette, pappardelle, penne, rigatoni, spaghetti, ziti. See pages 12–13.

pastry recipes

shortcrust pastry
2 cups plain (all-purpose) flour
155g (5 oz) butter, chopped
iced water
Process the flour and butter in a food processor until fine crumbs have formed. Add enough iced water to form a soft dough, remove from the food processor and knead lightly. Wrap the dough in plastic wrap and refrigerate for 30 minutes before rolling to stop shrinkage of the pastry when cooked. Makes 500g (1 lb).

sweet shortcrust pastry
Add 3 tablespoons of caster (superfine) sugar in the first step of the recipe above to make sweet shortcrust pastry.

polenta
See page 70.

prosciutto
An Italian ham that has been salted then air-dried for up to 2 years. The paper-thin slices are eaten raw or used to flavour cooked dishes. Substitute with thinly sliced unsmoked bacon.

ramekins
See tins, moulds and baking dishes.

removable-base tart tins
See tins, moulds and baking dishes.

rice flour
A fine flour made from ground white rice. It is used in baking and in Asian cooking to coat foods.

rice wine
See page 110.

rosewater
An extract made by distilling rose petals in water, used throughout India and the Middle East in sweets and drinks. Available from health food stores and delicatessens.

sesame oil
See page 111.

shortcrust pastry
See pastry recipes.

small soup pasta
See page 13 (short).

springform pans
See tins, moulds and baking dishes.

star anise
A star-shaped spice used in Asian and Indian cooking for its sweet aniseed flavour. The whole spice and a powder are available from Asian food stores.

stock

beef stock

1.5 kg (3 lb) beef bones, cut
   into pieces
2 onions, quartered
2 carrots, quartered
2 stalks celery, cut into large pieces
assorted fresh herbs
2 bay leaves
10 peppercorns
4 litres (16 cups/128 fl oz) water
Bake the bones on a tray in a preheated 220°C (425°F) oven for 30 minutes. Add the onions and carrots and bake for 20 minutes. Transfer the bones, onions and carrots to a stockpot or large saucepan. Add the remaining ingredients and 2 cups (16 fl oz) boiling water. Bring to the boil and simmer for 4–5 hours, skimming the top regularly. Strain the stock and use, or refrigerate for up to 3 days or freeze for up to 3 months. Makes 2.5–3 litres (10–12 cups/ 80–96 fl oz).

chicken stock

1.5 kg (3 lb) chicken bones,
   cut into pieces
2 onions, quartered
2 carrots, quartered
2 stalks celery, cut into large pieces
assorted fresh herbs
2 bay leaves
10 peppercorns
4 litres (16 cups/128 fl oz) water
Place all the ingredients in a stockpot or large saucepan and simmer for 3–4 hours, skimming the top regularly. Strain and use or refrigerate for up to 3 days or freeze for up to 3 months. Makes 2.5–3 litres (10–12 cups/80–96 fl oz). For a brown chicken stock, brush the chicken bones with a little oil and roast for 30 minutes. Add the vegetables and roast for a further 25 minutes before making the stock.

fish stock

1 tablespoon butter
1 onion, finely chopped
750g (1½ lb) fish bones, chopped
1 cup (8 fl oz) white wine
1 litre (32 fl oz) water
10 peppercorns
3–4 sprigs mild herbs
1 bay leaf
Cook the butter and onion in a large saucepan over low heat for 10 minutes or until the onion is soft but not browned. Add the remaining ingredients and simmer for 20 minutes. Skim the top regularly. Strain and use or refrigerate for up to 2 days or freeze for up to 2 months. Makes 3–3½ cups (24–28 fl oz).
Note: Do not simmer this stock for more than 20 minutes or it will sour.

vegetable stock

4 litres (16 cups/128 fl oz) water
1 parsnip
2 onions, quartered
1 clove garlic, peeled
2 carrots, quartered
300g (10 oz) roughly chopped cabbage
3 stalks celery, cut into large pieces
small bunch mixed fresh herbs
2 bay leaves
1 tablespoon peppercorns
Place all the ingredients in a stockpot or large saucepan and simmer for 2 hours, skimming the top regularly. Strain and use, or refrigerate for up to 4 days or freeze for up to 8 months. Makes 2.5–3 litres (10–12 cups/80–96 fl oz).

sweet shortcrust pastry
See pastry recipes.

tahini
A thick, smooth and oily paste made from toasted and ground sesame seeds. Available in jars from health food stores and most supermarkets.

tins, moulds and baking dishes

dariole moulds
Small cylindrical metal or plastic moulds with slightly sloping sides. Used to hold mousses, jellies, crème caramel and other desserts.

ovenproof dishes
Usually made from glazed ceramic. Always check suitability for use in an oven before buying.

ramekins
Small ovenproof dishes usually made from porcelain and used to cook and serve dishes like soufflés, crème brûlées and fruit crumbles.

removable-base tart tins
Metal tart tins with fluted sides. The fluting doubles the surface area exposed to the heat, which speeds the cooking of pastry. The removable base makes unmoulding easier.

springform pans
A round cake tin with a removable side; unbuckle the clip and lift the ring from the base. Used for fragile or soft-topped cakes that need to be unmoulded without inverting.

vegetable stock
See stock.

wasabi paste
A pungent traditional Japanese condiment made from horseradish. Available from Asian food stores.

conversion chart

1 teaspoon = 5 ml
1 Australian tablespoon = 20 ml
  (4 teaspoons)
1 UK tablespoon = 15 ml
  (3 teaspoons/1/2 fl oz)
1 cup = 250 ml (8 fl oz)

liquid conversions

metric	imperial	US cups
30 ml	1 fl oz	1/8 cup
60 ml	2 fl oz	1/4 cup
80 ml	23/4 fl oz	1/3 cup
125 ml	4 fl oz	1/2 cup
185 ml	6 fl oz	3/4 cup
250 ml	8 fl oz	1 cup
375 ml	12 fl oz	11/2 cups
500 ml	16 fl oz	2 cups
600 ml	20 fl oz	21/2 cups
750 ml	24 fl oz	3 cups
1 litre	32 fl oz	4 cups

cup measures

1 cup almond meal	110g	31/2 oz
1 cup breadcrumbs, fresh	50g	2 oz
1 cup sugar, brown	200g	61/2 oz
1 cup sugar, white	225g	7 oz
1 cup caster (superfine) sugar	225g	7 oz
1 cup cornflour (cornstarch)	100g	31/2 oz
1 cup flour, plain and self-raising (self-rising)	125g	4 oz
1 cup icing (confectioner's) sugar	125g	4 oz
1 cup rice flour	100g	31/2 oz
1 cup rice, cooked	165g	51/2 oz
1 cup short-grain rice, uncooked	220g	7 oz
1 cup arborio/carnaroli rice, uncooked	220g	7 oz
1 cup basmati rice, uncooked	220g	7 oz
1 cup couscous, uncooked	180g	6 oz
1 cup lentils, du puy, uncooked	220g	7 oz
1 cup lentils, red, uncooked	200g	61/2 oz
1 cup polenta, fine, uncooked	180g	6 oz
1 cup rolled oats, uncooked	100g	31/2 oz
1 cup basil leaves	45g	11/2 oz
1 cup coriander (cilantro) leaves	40g	11/4 oz
1 cup mint leaves	35g	11/4 oz
1 cup parsley leaves, flat-leaf	40g	11/4 oz
1 cup cashews, whole	150g	5 oz
1 cup cooked chicken, pork or beef, shredded	150g	5 oz
1 cup olives	175g	6 oz
1 cup parmesan cheese, finely grated	100g	31/2 oz
1 cup peas, frozen	170g	51/2 oz
1 cup soybeans, frozen	150g	5 oz

index